# The gospel — did Paul and Jesus agree?

# The gospel —
# did Paul and Jesus agree?

## Peter Barnes

 EVANGELICAL PRESS

EVANGELICAL PRESS
12 Wooler Street, Darlington, Co. Durham, DL1 1RQ, England


© Evangelical Press 1994
*First published 1994*


**British Library Cataloguing in Publication data available**


ISBN 085234 325 6

Printed and bound in Great Britain by the Bath Press, Bath, Avon

# Contents

# 1.
# Jesus and Paul:
# an introduction

In 1906, in the aftermath of Russia's defeat by Japan in the war of 1905, the magisterial Russian novelist Leo Tolstoy, in a fit of anti-Semitic patriotism, lamented, 'I should like to write something to prove how the teachings of Christ, who was not a Jew, were replaced by the very different teachings of the apostle Paul, who was a Jew.'[1] Mercifully, Tolstoy never seems to have written such a work but, in one form or another, it has become widely accepted that Paul departed radically from the teachings of Jesus. The liberal German New Testament scholar Wilhelm Wrede has ventured the oft-quoted view that the apostle Paul was 'the second founder of Christianity'.[2] He added, 'This second founder of Christianity has even, compared with the first, exercised beyond all doubt the stronger — not the better — influence.'[3] Earlier, Ernest Renan had written that 'True Christianity, which will last for ever, comes from the Gospels, not from the epistles of Paul.'[4]

This raises what ought to be an obviously crucial issue. Leaving aside the anonymous epistle to the Hebrews, thirteen of the New Testament's twenty-seven books were written by the apostle Paul. If Paul misunderstood and corrupted the teachings of Jesus, then much of the New Testament must be rejected as unreliable. Among many modern scholars such a conclusion is firmly rejected — but for the wrong reasons. Robert Morgan thinks that 'The New Testament authors disagree in their theologies.'[5] James D. G. Dunn asserts that there were conservative and liberal views within the church from the very beginning, and that 'The earliest churches had no conception of the Jesus-tradition as something fixed, a body of tradition whose content and outline was firmly established from the first.'[6] This approach is in harmony with the modern view that there is no such thing as objective truth. Hence Paul's theology is portrayed, not as right or wrong, but as simply different from the other apostolic presentations. Each generation has the fallen desire to distort the teachings of Paul and recreate them after its own image.

The situation today reflects the confusion of modern society. There is considerable popular support for the prevailing scholarly view that there are many truths and many valid theologies, and that these are complementary, not contradictory. On the other hand, there are still many who separate Paul from Jesus, and think that the former distorted the teachings of the latter. And, of course, consistency is not always to be looked for — people who declare there is no such thing as absolute truth are absolutely sure that Paul was wrong!

## Some critical considerations

Those who are convinced that the Bible is what it says it is — the Word of God — may not feel the need to raise the issue of critical considerations. But at least it ought to be clear from the outset what is the approach of the present study. A number of points need to be made.

1. We do not know when the four Gospels were written, nor do we know in what form they were transmitted in the early days. Many narratives seem to have been written but not to have survived (see Luke 1:1). Paul certainly had access to information which is not in the four Gospels. For example, he knew that the resurrected Christ had appeared to over five hundred brethren at one time (1 Cor. 15:6) — but this episode is not directly referred to in the Gospels, although John Wenham thinks this could be linked to the episode in

Matthew 28:16-20.[7] Somehow or another — through word of mouth, a written source unknown to us, or perhaps by direct revelation from the Lord himself — Paul knew not only that the risen Christ had appeared to his followers, but that he had appeared to over five hundred of them.

Acts 20:35 also cites the Lord Jesus as saying, 'It is more blessed to give than to receive.' This saying is not found in the canonical Gospels, and may well indicate the existence of either unwritten sayings or other Gospels which contained authentic information about Christ. It is simply guesswork to pontificate about the earlier forms of our present Gospels. We do not know, and cannot know, whether Paul possessed them as we have them today.

Werner Georg Kümmel estimates that Matthew was written about A.D. 80-100, Mark about A.D. 70, and Luke around A.D. 70-90.[8] But these widely accepted dates rest on not much more than sophisticated, and usually rationalistic, guesswork. There is precious little reason to contest John Wenham's view that the three Synoptic Gospels were all written before the year A.D. 55, with Matthew being dated perhaps as early as A.D. 40.[9] John A. T. Robinson, hardly a theological conservative, also set out to show that the whole New Testament should be dated much earlier than most liberal critics would allow, and dated John's Gospel between A.D. 65-70.[10] In fact, there seems to be little reason why it may not be dated even earlier. F. F. Bruce was sure that Paul did not have access to the Gospels as we have them, but that is hardly one of life's certainties.[11] Paul possessed slabs of Gospel material, and may well have possessed a Gospel in its entirety — or even more than one.

2. John is regarded as a reliable Gospel, and Paul is regarded as the author of the Pastoral Epistles (1 and 2 Timothy and Titus) as well as other epistles which are sometimes disputed by critical scholars (e.g. Ephesians and Colossians).

3. Dogmatism is inappropriate, but Hebrews is not regarded as Pauline (perhaps, as Luther suggested, Apollos was the author).

4. Acts is regarded as authentic history, but this will not figure prominently in this study.

Such an approach will be viewed as novel, if not naïve, in some circles, but evangelical scholars have replied more than adequately to the unbelief of those who reject the reliability of the New Testament.[12] In fact, one of the most cogent and sensible criticisms of the so-called 'assured results of biblical scholarship' has come from the pen of C. S. Lewis. Lewis was steeped in the study of literature, and wrote bluntly of the critics of the Bible: 'I distrust them as critics.'[13] He noted, among other things, how often reviewers had reconstructed the genesis of his own books — and got it all wrong! These reviewers failed, despite having the overwhelming advantages of living in something like the same mental, spiritual, linguistic and cultural climate as Lewis himself. Modern biblical critics, of course, have no such advantages. Lewis adds, as a further illustration, that 'The huge essays in my own field which reconstruct the history of *Piers Plowman* or *The Faerie Queene* are most unlikely to be anything but sheer illusions.'[14]

The ardent belief in liberal biblical criticism which prevails in so many seminaries and universities today is a superstition which has done incalculable harm. The 'science', if it can be called such, is based on anti-Christian presuppositions, and has hindered, not enhanced, critical thinking. Furthermore, as Lewis commented with regard to the unbelieving clergy in his own Anglican communion, 'Missionary to the priests of one's own church is an embarrassing role; though I have a horrid feeling that if such mission work is not soon undertaken the future history of the Church of England is likely to be short.'[15] Those prophetic words were uttered back in 1959.

It would be worthwhile now to raise some issues where Paul is often perceived to be at odds with his divine Master.

**Everlasting punishment**

There is a widespread feeling, which is rarely argued cogently, that
Paul taught a doctrine of hell-fire and judgement while Jesus
preached mercy and love. A look at the evidence is very revealing.
It is Jesus who taught most clearly that those who refuse to respond
to him with saving faith will endure the most awful punishment for
all eternity.

In the parable of Lazarus and the rich man (if it is a parable),
Christ portrays hell as a place of terrible and final torment — even
a drop of water on the tongue would provide some relief for the
damned (Luke 16:23-26). Therefore we ought not to fear men, who
can kill our bodies, but that is all they can do. We ought to fear God
who can destroy both body and soul in hell (Matt. 10:28). Hell is
truly horrific — it is worse than being mutilated (Matt. 5:27-30). It
is a place where there is 'weeping and gnashing of teeth' (Matt. 8:12;
13:42, 50; 22:13; 25:30) and 'an everlasting fire created for the devil
and his angels' (Matt. 25:41). Here it is said of the damned that
'Their worm does not die and the fire is not quenched' (Mark 9:48).
The wrath of God abides on the disobedient for ever (John 3:36).

Paul is thankful that Jesus 'delivers us from the wrath to come'
(1 Thess. 1:10) for when the Lord comes again he will take
vengeance on those who do not know God and who do not obey the
gospel (2 Thess. 1:8). 'These shall be punished with everlasting
destruction from the presence of the Lord and from the glory of his
power' (2 Thess. 1:9). What Paul tells us is sobering enough, but it
is our Lord who portrays most graphically what it means to be cast
off from God's mercy for all eternity. Dante's *Inferno* drew more
from the words of Christ than from the apostle Paul.


**Anti-Semitism**

It is a sad fact that Jews have often suffered much at the hands of
some who professed to be Christians. When the Crusaders recap-
tured Jerusalem in 1099, the streets were reported to be ankle-deep

in blood. Sometimes the apostle Paul is blamed as the one ultimately responsible for promoting such hatred and oppression. This issue has become especially sensitive since the Holocaust under the Nazis during World War II. Indeed, so sensitive is it that when Paul writes that Jews killed the Lord Jesus and their own prophets and have persecuted Christians (1 Thess. 2:14-16), a scholar as cautious as F. F. Bruce can declare such sentiments to be 'incongruous' and probably inauthentic.[16]

It is clear that the apostle Paul was no anti-Semite. He sought to present the whole counsel of God, without any compromise, in a way that did not needlessly offend any, Jew or Gentile (cf. 1 Cor. 9:19-23; 10:32-33). To keep the peace at Jerusalem, Paul was prepared to enter the temple to make sacrifices for four men who had taken vows (Acts 21:23-26; see also Acts 18:18). As F. F. Bruce comments, more aptly this time, 'Truly emancipated souls are not in bondage to their emancipation.'[17]

Paul could be vehement against the 'dogs' who undermined the gospel of free grace in Christ by preaching the necessity of circumcision for salvation (see Galatians; Phil. 3:2). But no one could be more flexible on secondary issues — hence Paul circumcized Timothy in order that he might proclaim Christ to the Jews (Acts 16:1-3). And no one could have had a greater love for his fellow-countrymen. Paul called himself 'a Hebrew of the Hebrews' (Phil. 3:5), and once uttered the extraordinary declaration: 'I could wish that I myself were accursed from Christ for my brethren, my kinsmen according to the flesh' (Rom. 9:3). Martin Luther comments that this is 'the strongest and utmost kind of love: utter self-hatred becomes the sign of the highest love for another'.[18] Only Moses' plea for his fellow Israelites, after the apostasy of the golden calf, can rival the depth of Paul's self-sacrificing love for his people. Moses begged the Lord, 'Yet now, if you will forgive their sin — but if not, I pray, blot me out of your book which you have written' (Exod. 32:32).

Paul's heart-desire and prayer for Israel was that they would be saved (Rom. 10:1). Far from repudiating Israel, Paul saw the Jews as the root of the olive tree, with the Gentiles as the branches (Rom.

11:16). Some of the 'natural branches' had been broken off, but this was done that the Gentiles might be grafted in (Rom. 11:21-22). In Christ, there is neither Jew nor Greek (Gal. 3:28). Anti-Semitism was far removed from Paul's character; Paul was in fact one of the most passionate lovers of the Jewish people that history has ever seen. In this he revealed the heart and mind of Christ, who wept over Jerusalem and yearned that God's ancient people might know the salvation to be wrought by their Messiah (Matt. 23:37-39; Luke 19:41-44).

## Feminism and sexuality

Sometimes Paul is portrayed as a feminist ahead of his times, but often he is derided as one who had no appreciation of women. Neither approach is faithful to Scripture, and both reveal a mind made up before the Bible is opened. Paul declares quite clearly that women are not to teach or rule over men in an official capacity in the church (1 Tim. 2:11-12). Both the Old and the New Testaments record that on occasions God used women prophets (e.g. Exod.15:20; Judg. 4:4; 2 Kings 22:14; Isa. 8:3; Acts 21:9). However, the *ordinary* offices of God's covenant community, as opposed to the *extraordinary* offices, were not open to women. Hence there could be no women priests or elders in Old Testament Israel (Exod.18:21,25; 29:1-37; Num.11:16-30) and no women elders in the New Testament church (1 Cor. 14:34; 1 Tim. 2:11-12).

This is widely disputed at the present time. The liberal Roman Catholic priest Wilfrid Harrington refers to 1 Timothy 2:11-14 as 'a sad passage', which must come from the pen of another writer besides Paul.[19] William Klassen also asserts that it does not belong to Paul, and adds that 'It is hard to measure the damage it has done in the history of the church.'[20] Back at the beginning of the third century, the fiery African Christian Tertullian declared that the heretic Marcion 'would rather call a passage an addition than explain it'.[21] The same propensity is very much alive today.

Although Paul himself was not married — at least not when he wrote 1 Corinthians 7:8 — he pictured the relationship between a man and his wife as similar to that between Christ and his church (Eph. 5:22-33). The husband is to give himself to the wife (v. 25), seek her welfare (vv. 26-7), love her as he does himself (v. 28), and care for her (v. 29). There is to be a mutuality in sexual relations; each spouse has rights over the other's body (1 Cor. 7:3-5). Women are not allowed to teach in the church meetings (1 Cor. 14:34), but in Christ there is neither male nor female (Gal. 3:28). Men and women do not have the same functions — and headship in church and family is clearly given to the male — but in worth before God there is complete equality.

Furthermore, Paul reveals much tenderness towards women who worked with him. He even commends two quarrelling women, Euodia and Syntyche, as those 'who have contended at my side in the cause of the gospel' (Phil. 4:2-3, NIV). Phoebe is warmly commended as a sister in the Lord and a servant — or a deacon, who neither taught nor governed, but ministered to the temporal needs of the saints in the church in Cenchrea (Rom. 16:1-2). In fact, Paul is most appreciative of the work and fellowship of a number of Christian women whose names are recorded in the last chapter of the epistle to the Romans (Rom. 16:3,6,12,13,15). It is just possible that in Romans 16:7 the name Junia refers to a woman apostle, which might be allowable as the term 'apostle', like 'prophet', described an extraordinary, not an ordinary, office in the church. Nevertheless, the name should probably be read as Junias, which is a man's name. In any case, it seems that Paul is simply saying that he (Junias) or she (Junia) was *well regarded by* the apostles, not that he or she was an apostle.

The only fair conclusion is that Paul was neither a feminist nor a misogynist; he neither sought to exalt women nor to suppress them. He was not afraid of human sexuality, nor did he idolize it. Women were not treated as honorary men, nor was their femininity assaulted. Equally ruined by the Fall, equally redeemed by Christ, equally called to Christian life and service, Christian women are nevertheless not permitted to rule or teach men from the eldership of Christ's church. In an age of slogans and shallow thinking, the apostle's voice is a sane and coherent call to return to the God-given order set out in Scripture and testified to through all human experience.

Nor is there any evidence that Jesus' attitude to feminism and sexuality was any different from that of Paul. The Gospel of Luke tells us that Jesus 'went through every city and village, preaching and bringing the glad tidings of the kingdom of God. And the twelve were with him, and certain women who had been healed of evil spirits and infirmities — Mary called Magdalene, out of whom had come seven demons, and Joanna the wife of Chuza, Herod's steward, and Susanna, and many others who provided for him from their substance' (Luke 8:1-3). Mark records that many women followed Jesus and ministered to him when he was in Galilee, and came up with him as he made his way to Jerusalem to be crucified (Mark 15:40-41).

Judaism could be harsh towards women. It could even be said, 'Sooner let the words of the Law be burnt than delivered to women.'[22] Not so with Christ. He commended Mary for leaving Martha with the cooking and serving while she sat at the Master's feet to hear his word. Martha earned a tender rebuke: 'Martha, Martha, you are worried and troubled about many things. But one thing is needed, and Mary has chosen that good part, which will not be taken away from her' (Luke 10:41-42). Women ministered to Jesus, and he clearly expected them to hear his word and follow it for themselves. But it remains self-evident that leadership in the emerging Christian community was not open to women. The twelve disciples were all men; it is strange that women were omitted if Jesus was, as William Klassen thinks,[23] a first-century feminist. It is also a desperate expedient to try to claim, let alone prove, that the seventy (or seventy-two) who were sent out two by two to preach and heal the sick were teams consisting of a man and a woman.[24] Both Paul and Jesus had a vital place for ministering women in the church, but not for women pastors and teachers.

So far as their attitude to sexuality is concerned, Paul and Jesus appear consistent with one another. Both saw a place for the one who remains single for the sake of the kingdom, and saw themselves in that category (Matt. 19:12; 1 Cor. 7:7,32-33). Jesus condemned adultery and fornication as sins which resulted from the corruption of the human heart (Matt. 15:19). In fact, the lust that led to such sins was said to be equivalent in God's eyes to the act itself, and required radical surgery: 'If your right eye causes you to sin, pluck it out and cast it from you; for it is more profitable for you that one of your members perish, than for your whole body to be cast into hell. And if your right hand causes you to sin, cut it off and cast it from you; for it is more profitable for you that one of your members perish, than for your whole body to be cast into hell' (Matt. 5:29-30). Jesus was not recommending self-mutilation but a decided dealing with sin. Evil is not to be trifled with!

Paul's writings reveal similar teachings to that of his Master. Paul warned the Corinthians — of some notoriety in the ancient world, where the verb *'korinthiazein'* meant 'to engage in debauchery' — that adulterers and fornicators who remained outside of the saving work of Christ through his Spirit would not inherit the kingdom of God (1 Cor. 6:9-11). Sexual immorality was a work of the flesh, not a fruit of the Holy Spirit (Gal. 5:19). Such things are not fitting even to be named among the saints (Eph. 5:3-4) for they arouse the judgement of God (Eph. 5:6; Col. 3:6; 1 Thess. 4:6).

Attempts to make Paul an exponent of sexual permissiveness in the name of freedom or harsh legalism in the name of law invariably fail. Like Jesus, Paul made it clear what sexual boundaries God had established for our good, but then offered the gospel of salvation by grace to sinners of whatever ilk (note Luke 7:36-50; John 8:1-11; and the wonderful grace expressed in 'such were some of you' in 1 Cor. 6:11).

In his teachings on everlasting punishment, the Jews, feminism and human sexuality, the apostle Paul reflected the mind of Christ, and can in no way be accused of distorting the Christian message.

## Some surface differences

Even a cursory reading of the Gospels and Paul's epistles reveals that some of the issues raised in Jesus' ministry are not taken up by

Paul. For example, Jesus referred to himself as the 'Son of Man' more often than he used any other title, even 'Son of God'. The Son of Man came in all lowliness, with no place to rest his head (Matt. 8:20), in order to give his life a ransom for many (Mark 10:45). Yet, as Daniel prophesied, there would be 'one like the Son of Man, coming with the clouds of heaven' whose dominion would be 'an everlasting dominion, which shall not pass away, and his kingdom the one which shall not be destroyed' (Dan. 7:13-14). It was when Jesus identified himself as this Son of Man that the high priest Caiaphas condemned him for blasphemy (Mark 14:61-64).

Perhaps surprisingly, Paul never refers to Jesus as the Son of Man. The apostle much prefers to describe Jesus as Lord. One can only speculate as to why he did this. It is possible that he feared that Gentile converts might not understand the full implications of the Son of Man title, although it must be said that Paul obviously expected Greek Christians to grasp quickly lessons drawn from the history of the Jews of the Old Testament (e.g. 1 Cor. 10:1-13). Whatever the case, it is significant that the non-Pauline epistles also fail to refer to Jesus as the Son of Man (outside the Gospels the term is only found in Acts 7:56 and Rev. 1:13; 14:14). However, it is possible, perhaps even probable, that the idea of the Son of Man is behind Paul's contrasting of the work of Adam and of Christ in Romans 5:12-21 and 1 Corinthians 15:20-28,42-49. Here Christ is shown to be the true man, or son of man, as portrayed in Psalm 8.

Something similar becomes apparent when we consider the term 'the kingdom of God' (or 'the kingdom of heaven'). After his baptism and his temptations by Satan, Jesus began to preach: 'The time is fulfilled, and the kingdom of God is at hand. Repent, and believe in the gospel' (Mark 1:15). The kingly rule of God was breaking into this fallen world in the coming of Jesus Christ as God's Son and the appointed King. Through repentance and faith in Christ, sinners could be accepted into that kingdom. Jesus explained the nature of the kingdom through his many parables, with their constant refrain: 'The kingdom of heaven is like ...' (e.g. Matt.13:31,33,44,45,47).

Paul, on the other hand, only used the expression 'the kingdom of God' eight times in his epistles. He declared that the kingdom was not about food and drink, but righteousness and peace and joy in the Holy Spirit (Rom. 14:17). The unrighteous will not inherit the kingdom (1 Cor. 6:9-10; Gal. 5:19-20), so the Christian must have a walk worthy of God who calls his people into his own kingdom and glory (1 Thess. 2:12). The kingdom is not something that Christians enter at some future date or in some supposed millennium, for God 'has delivered us from the power of darkness and translated us into the kingdom of the Son of his love' (Col. 1:13). The kingdom has yet to be consummated, but it is here already to those with saving faith in Christ.

Again, it is only speculation, but it may be that Paul hesitated to use the term 'the kingdom of God' too often because he feared that it might be misunderstood by the imperial authorities in a political sense, as happened in Jesus' day (Luke 19:11; John 6:15). Certainly, that misunderstanding did arise in Paul's proclamation of the gospel at Thessalonica (see Acts 17:7). Or, it may be that, as at Corinth, there were Christians who thought that being members of God's kingdom meant that they were already kings here on earth, and that the way of the cross was beneath them. Paul once wrote with powerful irony to the Corinthians, 'You are already full! You are already rich! You have reigned as kings without us — and indeed I could wish you did reign, that we also might reign with you!' (1 Cor. 4:8). For whatever reason, Paul favoured the expression 'in Christ': 'If anyone is in Christ, he is a new creation; old things have passed away; behold, all things have become new' (2 Cor. 5:17). The expression 'in Christ' or 'in the Lord' is used by Paul about 164 times.

There are issues which are quite major in Jesus' ministry which barely arise in that of Paul. Jesus ran into constant trouble with the Pharisees over his healing of people on the Sabbath (Matt. 12:1-14; John 9:16). It was because Jesus healed on the Sabbath and because he claimed to be equal with God that the Jews sought to kill him (John 5:16-18). But the issue is scarcely raised in Paul's letters. Paul writes, 'One person esteems one day above another; another esteems every day alike. Let each be fully convinced in his own mind' (Rom. 14:5). Paul is critical of those who make an issue of observing holy days and seasons (Gal. 4:9-10; Col. 2:16) for this can easily undermine our trust in the sufficiency of Christ's work for sinners.

But if Paul rarely refers to the Sabbath, he has to maintain a firm stand on the subject of circumcision — a subject which apparently did not surface during the time of Christ's public ministry. Circumcision is profitable only if it is accompanied by the spiritual circumcision of our sinful hearts (Rom. 2:25-29). It did not justify Abraham in God's sight, for he was justified before he was circumcised (Rom. 4:9-12). Circumcision is nothing compared to being a new creation in Christ (Gal. 6:15), faith working through love (Gal. 5:6) and keeping God's commandments (1 Cor. 7:19). Circumcision had its God-given purpose to fulfil (Rom. 3:1-2), but to trust in the fact that one is circumcised — like trusting in the fact that one is baptized — is to fall from the grace of God in Christ (Gal. 5:2-4).

One would hardly expect the controversies fought in Paul's day to be the same as those fought during Jesus' public ministry. Jesus was working among Jews steeped in the Old Testament; Paul went first to the synagogues, but many of his converts came out of Gentile backgrounds. Surface differences such as those just discussed are no evidence of a deep division between Paul and Jesus.

## Two different spheres

The most significant difference between Jesus and Paul can be located in the two different spheres in which they worked: for the most part, Jesus looked ahead to his death and resurrection while Paul looked back to those two great events. As Albert Schweitzer put it, 'Both are looking towards the same mountain range, but whereas Jesus sees it as lying before Him, Paul already stands upon it and its first slopes are already behind him.'[25] Jesus spoke of a time when some of those standing before him would not taste death till they saw the kingdom of God come with power (Mark 9:1). He was looking *ahead* to his own resurrection, and what followed that — his ascension to the right hand of the Father and the descent of the Holy Spirit. Paul, however, wrote that Christ was 'declared to be the Son of God with power, according to the Spirit of holiness, by the resurrection from the dead' (Rom. 1:4). He was looking *back* to what had taken place in Christ's rising from the dead, never to die again. Paul was writing 'when the fulness of the time had come' (Gal. 4:4); the wondrous work of redemption had been accomplished; the kingdom was not only at hand, it had been inaugurated. Christ was looking to the victory he *would win*; Paul was looking to the victory Christ *had won*.

# 2.
# Paul's view of his own authority

## A man of two worlds

The apostle Paul was known as Saul earlier in his career. He was
born in Tarsus in Cilicia (Acts 9:11; 21:39; 22:3), of the tribe of
Benjamin, and was 'a Hebrew of the Hebrews' (Phil. 3:5), but he
was also born a Roman citizen (Acts 16:37-38; 22:25-29). He was
thus a man who became familiar with two worlds — Pharisaic
orthodoxy and Greek cosmopolitanism. Studying under Gamaliel I,
a grandson of the more liberal Hillel, Paul came to Jerusalem (Acts
22:3) and became very zealous for the law (Gal. 1:14). But he also
knew Greek authors, and could quote them when necessary (Acts
17:28; 1 Cor. 15:33; Titus 1:12).

## Weak but strong

As a man, Paul was not very imposing physically — indeed, his
physical presence was said to be weak (2 Cor. 10:10). At the
backwater of Lystra, the native people thought he was the messen-
ger god Hermes, in contrast to Barnabas, whose larger size made
him resemble Zeus (Acts 14:12). There is an apocryphal description
of Paul from the second century which portrays him as 'a man small
of stature, with a bald head and crooked legs, in a good state of body,

with eyebrows meeting and nose somewhat hooked, full of friend-
liness; for now he appeared like a man, and now he had the face of
an angel'.[1] This is unflattering enough to be authentic.

Physically, Paul may not have been an awesome figure, but he
endured extraordinary hardships in order to take the gospel out into
the known world. He suffered from whippings, beatings, a stoning,
three shipwrecks, difficult journeys, danger from brigands, threats
from Jews, Gentiles and false Christians, as well as weariness,
hunger, thirst, cold, and nakedness (2 Cor. 11:24-27). Added to this
may have been an eye problem. That, at least, is the implication that
is usually drawn from his reference to the physical infirmity that led
him to preach the gospel in Galatia. Paul says that he was so well
received that he considered that the Galatians would have plucked
out their own eyes and given them to him, if that were possible (Gal.
4:13-15).

In 2 Corinthians, Paul says that he prayed to the Lord three times
to be delivered from a 'thorn in the flesh' that was causing him a
measure of discomfort (2 Cor. 12:7-10). There is a temptation to
read our own diseases and afflictions into this passage; and the
'thorn' has been understood to refer to opposition, malaria, recur-
rent earache or headache, epilepsy, or perhaps the same eye problem
that beset him in Galatia. Whatever the case, Paul knew what it was
to suffer from physical ailments.


**The preacher**

Surprisingly enough, Paul was not naturally a skilful orator; he was
not capable of turning on the verbal fireworks after the manner of a
Demosthenes or Cicero. Paul reminded the Corinthians that he had
not come to them with 'excellence of speech or of wisdom'. In fact,
his speech and his preaching were 'not with persuasive words of
human wisdom, but in demonstration of the Spirit and of power'.
This was so that their faith would not be in the wisdom of men but
in the power of God (1 Cor. 2:1-5). When his enemies declared that
his speech was contemptible — as opposed to his weighty letters —

Paul did not deny the charge, but went on to assert, 'Even though I am untrained in speech, yet I am not in knowledge' (2 Cor. 10:10; 11:6).

A preacher is not necessarily an orator. Paul even managed to extend one Sunday night message beyond the bounds of one young man's endurance, which led to a deep sleep and a dangerous fall, but thankfully a happy ending! (Acts 20:7-12). The church has possessed great orators — John Chrysostom was known as 'John with the golden mouth' and Augustine of Hippo was Professor of Rhetoric at Milan University before his conversion. But there is the other side too — Richard Sibbes suffered from a lisp and a stammer; Thomas Chalmers rarely moved and used to follow his manuscript with his finger; early in his career Jonathan Edwards used to stare at the bell-rope at the back of the church; while George Whitefield, the greatest preacher England ever heard, had to overcome a squint. As a preacher, Paul possessed striking power and authority, but it was of God's Spirit, not of man's ability.

## Paul's authority as an apostle

Throughout his epistles, Paul wrote with the self-conscious authority of an apostle of Jesus Christ — one who had seen the risen Lord (1 Cor. 9:1-2), who had been directly commissioned by him (Gal. 1:1), and who was able to perform apostolic signs and wonders (2 Cor. 12:12). To the Galatians, Paul wrote most emphatically that there is only one gospel (Gal. 1:6-7). All roads might have led to Rome in the ancient world, but they did not — and do not — lead to heaven. Paul asserts, 'But even if we, or an angel from heaven, preach any other gospel to you than what we have preached to you, let him be accursed' (Gal. 1:8). Lest we think this was simply a cantankerous slip from an otherwise ecumenical pen, Paul repeats his assertion in the next verse: 'As we have said before, so now I say again, if anyone preaches any other gospel to you than what you have received, let him be accursed' (Gal. 1:9).

No doubt Paul obtained some of his information about Christ

from the other apostles, but he always claimed an authority which was not dependent on any man. As he informed the Galatians, 'But I make known to you, brethren, that the gospel which was preached by me is not according to man. For I neither received it from man, nor was I taught it, but it came through the revelation of Jesus Christ' (Gal. 1:11-12). Paul could only have obtained his gospel from God because of the following reasons:

1. His past in Judaism only led him to zealously persecute the Christian church (Gal. 1:13-14).
2. His conversion to Christ could only have been a result of God's predestinating grace (Gal.1:15-16).
3. He barely knew the other apostles, living, for the most part, some distance from them (Gal. 1:16-24).

Hence Paul claimed an authority which was divine because it came direct from God — Father, Son and Holy Spirit.

When Paul wrote to the exuberant Corinthians about their overevaluation of the gift of tongues, he did not mince his words. He was not negotiating: 'If anyone thinks himself to be a prophet or spiritual, let him acknowledge that the things which I write to you are the commandments of the Lord' (1 Cor. 14:37). Paul claimed to have the mind of Christ (1 Cor. 2:16) and to teach that which the Spirit teaches (1 Cor. 2:13). Hence Paul could write, as he did to the Thessalonians, 'For this reason we also thank God without ceasing, because when you received the word of God which you heard from us, you welcomed it not as the word of men, but as it is in truth, the word of God' (1 Thess. 2:13).

Just as God gave commandments to Moses, so Christ gave commandments to Paul. Sexual purity, for example, forms part of the commandments which Paul gave the Thessalonians through the Lord Jesus (1 Thess. 4:2). This is the will of God ( 1 Thess. 4:3), and the one who rejects this does not reject man but God (1 Thess. 4:8). On the apparently more mundane issue of manual work, Paul issued not discussion points for debate, but commands which required obedience (2 Thess. 3:4,6,10,12,14). Paul is fond of using a military

word (*'parangelia'*, 1 Thess. 4:2; 1 Tim. 1:18) which is used else-
where to describe the way a superior officer would issue orders to
those under him. In Acts 16:24, for example, the magistrates
charged the Philippian jailer to place Paul and Silas in the inner
prison and to fasten their feet in the stocks. It was a charge to be
obeyed, not a possible course of action to be entertained. Paul wrote
with this same self-conscious authority as an apostle appointed by
the Lord Jesus Christ.

To accept or reject Paul's gospel is a matter of everlasting life or
death (2 Cor. 2:14-16). Only those whom the god of this world has
blinded will refuse to see the light of Paul's gospel. Such people are
perishing (2 Cor. 4:3-4). Paul's desire was, however, quite different:
'Therefore I write these things being absent, lest being present I
should use sharpness, according to the authority which the Lord has
given me for edification and not for destruction' (2 Cor. 13:10). Paul
spoke as an ambassador for Christ, as one through whom God
pleaded and Christ implored, that sinners might be reconciled to
God (2 Cor. 5:20). And, as the Lord himself said, 'He who hears you
hears me, he who rejects you rejects me, and he who rejects me
rejects him who sent me' (Luke 10:16). Christ can only be known
through the writings of his apostles; there is no other way of
knowing him.

It is noteworthy that Paul's claims were accepted by the other
apostles. Paul had his disagreements with Peter, and once had to
withstand him to his face because Peter, fearing the Jews, was
withdrawing from the Gentiles (Gal. 2:11-14). But near the end of
his life, Peter wrote to commend Paul as 'our beloved brother'
whose epistles were to receive the obedient respect due to the rest
of the Scriptures (2 Peter 3:15-16).

## A humble servant

While Paul saw himself as an apostle with definite authority granted
by Christ himself, he also saw himself as a servant. These two
strands in his thinking are by no means contradictory, although they

are often seen to be so by many scholars today. Just as Christ is both Lord and servant of his people (John 13:13-14), so too Paul could be both apostle and minister.

Not unlike many churches today, the Corinthian church in the first century succumbed to a personality cult. Different parties within the church began to favour different preachers, even though these preachers proclaimed the same gospel of salvation by grace. They seem to have lined up into four groups: one the followers of Paul, one of Apollos, one of Cephas (Peter), and one (perhaps the most pretentious of all) of Christ (1 Cor. 1:12). On one occasion at Haverhill in Suffolk in the nineteenth century Charles Spurgeon arrived at the chapel to find that his grandfather was already in the pulpit and preaching to the congregation. When the old man saw young Spurgeon, he said, 'Here comes my grandson! He may preach the gospel better than I can, but he cannot preach a better gospel.'[2] The Corinthians of Paul's day were not so discerning.

As a result, Paul had to correct the carnal thinking of his new converts: 'Who then is Paul, and who is Apollos, but ministers [or servants] through whom you believed, as the Lord gave to each one?' (1 Cor. 3:5). Later he was to state, 'For we do not preach ourselves, but Christ Jesus the Lord, and ourselves your servants for Jesus' sake' (2 Cor. 4:5). In this, Paul reflected the mind of Christ, who had told his disciples, 'You know that those who are considered rulers over the Gentiles lord it over them, and their great ones exercise authority over them. Yet it shall not be so among you; but whoever desires to become great among you shall be your servant. And whoever of you desires to be first shall be slave of all. For even the Son of Man did not come to be served, but to serve, and to give his life a ransom for many' (Mark 10:42-45). Paul was gentle with his converts, just as a nursing mother cherishes her children (1 Thess. 2:7).

Paul could go so far as to say he was nothing: 'So then neither he who plants is anything, nor he who waters, but God who gives the increase' (1 Cor. 3:7). Yet at the same time he and his colleagues were 'God's fellow workers' (1 Cor. 3:9). Paul directed his converts to look to Christ, not himself. As Charles Wesley was to put it,

Sweetly may we all agree,
Touched with softest sympathy;
There is neither bond nor free,
Great nor servile, Lord, in thee:
Love, like death, hath all destroyed,
Rendered all distinctions void;
Names and sects and parties fall,
Thou, O Christ, art all in all.[3]

George Whitefield was equally convinced, but less poetic: 'What is Calvin, or what is Luther? Let us look above names and parties; let Jesus ... be our all in all.'[4]

## Restraint in exercising authority

While Paul had no doubts about his apostolic authority, he did not fall into the trap of issuing commandments every time he opened his mouth. For example, he very much wanted Apollos to go back to work among the Corinthians, but Apollos disagreed. Paul made his views known, but they could not be enforced on a point of strategy, as opposed to a matter of doctrinal or ethical revelation: 'Now concerning our brother Apollos, I strongly urged him to come to you with the brethren, but he was quite unwilling to come at this time; however, he will come when he has a convenient time' (1 Cor. 16:12). I once met an unemployed man in a city in a rural part of New South Wales in Australia. This man had left his job and home in another part of the country and moved many hundreds of miles to his new city, where he had found nothing much to do for some four or five months. Such a move was undertaken, so my friend explained, because his pastor had experienced what he considered was 'a word from the Lord' that this man should leave one place and go to another. Clearly, this pastor was claiming authority which was beyond that claimed by the apostle Paul himself in 1 Corinthians 16:12! There is a similar restraint in the letter to Philemon, where Paul pleads with the slave-owner not to demand the return of his runaway slave Onesimus, who had become a Christian. Paul wrote, 'Therefore, though I might be very bold in Christ to command you what is fitting, yet for love's sake I rather appeal to you — being such a one as Paul, the aged, and now also a prisoner of Jesus Christ — I appeal to you for my son Onesimus, whom I have begotten while in my chains, who once was unprofitable to you, but now is profitable to you and to me' (Philem. 8-11). Paul wanted to keep Onesimus with him, but did not want to do anything without Philemon's consent, that Philemon's good deed 'might not be by compulsion, as it were, but voluntary' (Philem. 13-14). Paul drops hints rather than issues orders: 'Having confidence in your obedience, I write to you, knowing that you will do even more than I say' (Philem. 21).

Paul might have stood on his apostolic authority, or he might have appealed to the words of Deuteronomy 23:15-16: 'You shall not give back to his master the slave who has escaped from his master to you. He may dwell with you in your midst, in the place which he chooses within one of your gates, where it seems best to him; you shall not oppress him.' Instead, as on the issue of giving (see 2 Cor. 9:7), Paul realized the worth of obedience freely given from the heart. Calvin drew a wise lesson from Paul's approach: 'By his example he [Paul] shows that pastors should endeavour to draw disciples gently rather than to drag them by force; and indeed, when, by condescending to entreaty, he foregoes his right, this has far greater power to obtain his wish than if he issued a command.'[5]

Paul had no love of authority for its own sake, to feed his own ego. He did not want to put a leash on anyone (1 Cor. 7:35). He did not order Christians to hand over their wealth to aid the cause of Christ's poor: 'I speak not by commandment' (2 Cor. 8:8). On the contrary, Paul simply gave his advice (2 Cor. 8:10). Hence the Christian preacher is not to be one who browbeats his people. There have been too many cases of a church's commanding where God has remained silent and remaining silent where God has spoken. Some churches have demanded that their ministers wear a certain kind of dress (despite what Christ says in Matt. 23:5-7), while others have insisted that the biblical warnings against drunkenness are actually warnings against alcohol as such (despite the miracle in John 2:1-

11). Yet there has often been a strange silence on the unfashionable issue of abortion (despite what David says about the living unborn child in Ps. 139:13-16).

Paul respected the capacity of his readers to think for themselves: 'I speak as to wise men; judge for yourselves what I say' (1 Cor. 10:15). The great apostle was no tyrant: 'Not that we have dominion over your faith, but are fellow workers for your joy; for by faith you stand' (2 Cor. 1:24). Paul wanted Christians to obey him, but to do so because of their faith in Christ. This would make obedience sweet, a delight and not a burden, a result of a heartfelt affection rather than an imposition of an outside will.

We find in Paul no heavy-handed assault upon the individuality of his converts; there is no attempt to make Pauline clones. It is sin that makes us conformists who lack originality; it is grace that makes us individuals who are nevertheless unified. John the Baptist was stern and ascetic, while Jesus was more social in outlook — but both were carrying out the will of the Father (Matt. 11:18-19). As C. S. Lewis put it, 'It is when I turn to Christ, when I give myself up to His Personality, that I first begin to have a real personality of my own.'[6]

In Paul's mind, there was no necessity to set out detailed rules of life for the Christian to obey. Paul's approach is exemplified in his epistle to the Philippians: 'All of us who are mature should take such a view of things. And if on some point you think differently, that too God will make clear to you. Only let us live up to what we have already attained' (Phil. 3:15-16, NIV). Paul could live with those who differed with him on the subject of food laws, holy days, or eating meat that had been offered to idols (see Rom. 14-15; 1 Cor. 8-10), provided they did not undermine the sufficiency of Christ's person and work for salvation (Gal. 4:10-11; Col. 2:16-23).

William Hendriksen's summary is an apt one: 'True religion, then, is a matter not of precept upon precept but of basic principles. These are few but very important. If by the light of God's special revelation these principles are consistently applied, then all the rest will follow. God will not refuse to give further light to him who walks by the light already given.'[7]

## Magnifying his office, not his person

Paul could be fierce against those who opposed the apostolic gospel of justification by faith (see Gal. 1:6-9), but was surprisingly mild towards those who opposed his person without rejecting his gospel. From his prison (probably while under house arrest in Rome), Paul wrote to the Philippians, 'It is true that some preach Christ out of envy and rivalry, but others out of good will. The latter do so in love, knowing that I am put here for the defence of the gospel. The former preach Christ out of selfish ambition, not sincerely, supposing that they can stir up trouble for me while I am in chains. But what does it matter? The important thing is that in every way, whether from false motives or true, Christ is preached. And because of this I rejoice' (Phil. 1:15-18, NIV).

At times Paul appeared to be almost indifferent as to how people responded to himself as a person. When confronted by opposition from some at Corinth, Paul stated, 'Now we pray to God that you will not do anything wrong. Not that people will see that we have stood the test but that you will do what is right even though we may seem to have failed' (2 Cor. 13:7, NIV). Minimizing his own person, Paul magnified his office as an apostle of Christ. Hence he wrote to the Corinthians, 'For I ought to have been commended by you; for in nothing was I behind the most eminent apostles, though I am nothing' (2 Cor. 12:11). Dislike of his person was one thing; repudiation of his apostleship was quite another. The former was regrettable, but in some sense tolerable; the latter was an affront to Christ.

That is why there is a paradoxical combination of abject humility and unyielding authority found in Paul's writings. He who never forgot his past as one who had blasphemed the Messiah and persecuted the church of God (1 Cor. 15:9; 1 Tim. 1:13-15) was nevertheless part of the apostolic foundation of the household of God (Eph. 2:20), one who had been entrusted by God with the mystery which had been held back in earlier times but which was now being openly revealed (Eph. 3:1-7).

Self-effacement thus went hand-in-hand with a clear sense of divine purpose in Paul's life. When confronted by threats to his authority and attacks upon his character at Corinth, Paul replied, 'We are not trying to commend ourselves to you again, but are giving you an opportunity to take pride in us, so that you can answer those who take pride in what is seen rather than in what is in the heart' (2 Cor. 5:12, NIV). Again, Calvin points out the lesson: 'We are here taught, that Christ's servants ought to be concerned as to their own reputation, only in so far as is for the advantage of the Church.'[8]

In summary, it can be said that Paul was authoritative but not authoritarian, restrained but not vacillating, humble but by no means weak. In his person, he knew that he was nothing more than a sinner saved by God's free grace in Christ; as an apostle, he knew he was God's chosen instrument to make known his revealed truth.

# 3.
# Paul's knowledge of Jesus' life

At first sight, it is surprising how little Paul does say about Jesus' life on earth. Rudolf Bultmann, the radical German biblical critic who died in 1976, makes the bizarre assertion that this was because Paul was not interested in Jesus' life. He wrote, 'All that is important for him [Paul] in the story of Jesus is the fact that Jesus was born a Jew and lived under the Law (Gal. 4:4) and that he had been crucified (Gal. 3:1; 1 Cor. 2:2; Phil. 2:5ff, etc).'[1] A closer look at the evidence will reveal that we can say much more than that. It is Bultmann, not Paul, who has no interest in the historical person of Jesus of Nazareth.

Paul mentions that Christ was born of the seed of David according to the flesh (Rom. 1:3), which is in harmony with the record of the Gospels (e.g. Matt. 1:1-17; 9:27). However, Paul gives no details about Jesus' birth itself. It is affirmed that 'When the fulness of the time had come, God sent forth his Son, born of a woman, born under the law' (Gal. 4:4). But, as J. Gresham Machen has pointed out,[2] this passage cannot be fairly used to support either the view that Paul believed in the virgin birth of Christ or that he did not believe it. Machen goes on to write, in his own restrained way, 'All that can be said is that as a matter of fact neither in this passage nor anywhere else in the Pauline Epistles does Paul mention the human father of Jesus.'[3] Paul simply never mentions the virgin birth of our Lord — but nothing he says contradicts what Matthew and Luke tell us about the supernatural way that God's eternal Son came to earth.

Paul knew something of Jesus' family life in that he mentions that James was the Lord's brother (Gal. 1:19). Matthew refers to James and three others — Joses (or Joseph), Simon and Judas — as well as various sisters (Matt. 13:55-56), so there is no discrepancy on this subject between Paul and the Gospel writers. Paul also knew that the Lord had called twelve men to be his apostles (1 Cor. 15:5; cf. Matt. 10:1-4). Little is said of Jesus' life, nor even of the details of his death. Paul does refer to the Lord's Supper, instituted on the night on which Christ was 'delivered up' — either by Judas' betrayal, or God the Father's decree, or both (1 Cor. 11:23-26). There are also a number of references to the fact that Jesus was put to death by means of the Roman penalty of crucifixion (1 Cor. 1:23; Gal. 3:1,13; 6:14; Eph. 2:16). At his trial our Lord appeared before the Roman governor Pontius Pilate (1 Tim. 6:13). Despite the form of execution, Paul was aware that the Jews were heavily involved in the condemnation of their Messiah (1 Thess. 2:14-15). But death was followed by the glorious resurrection, the defeat of the last enemy itself (e.g. 1 Cor. 15).

Occasionally, in the course of presenting his case, Paul indicates, almost in passing, that he had access to more information than he needed to use in his epistles. For example, in arguing that he had the right to take with him on his missionary journeys a Christian wife — a right he never made use of — Paul asked, 'Do we have no right to take along a believing wife, as do also the other apostles, the brothers of the Lord, and Cephas?' (1 Cor. 9:5). The Gospels tell us that Jesus once healed Peter's mother-in-law (Mark 1:29-31) — an unplanned confirmation of the reliability of Paul's information.

Having said that, it must be acknowledged that Paul does not refer to the baptism of Jesus, the temptations (but see Heb. 2:18; 4:15), the calling of the disciples, the parables, the miracles (although the fact that Paul himself was used to perform mighty signs and wonders, as Rom. 15:18-19 and 2 Cor. 12:12 testify, surely implies that he knew that his Master performed even greater miracles), the transfiguration (note 2 Peter 1:16-18), the agony of Gethsemane (see Heb. 5:7-8), the events leading up to the cruci-fixion, or the figures of Mary, John the Baptist, or Judas. This is somewhat startling, but it ought not to excuse the kind of scholarly imbecility that we find, for instance, in Günther Bornkamm's claim that 'One may confidently affirm what many may find surprising and a paradox, that in spite of the almost two thousand years' interval, we today probably know more about the Jesus of history than did Paul.'[4]

In confronting his opponents at Ephesus, Paul wrote decisively to young Timothy that 'If anyone teaches otherwise and does not consent to wholesome words, even the words of our Lord Jesus Christ, and to the doctrine which is according to godliness, he is proud, [and knows] nothing' (1 Tim. 6:3-4). There is a clear implication here that Paul had access to Jesus' words, and also that his readers knew those words and were expected to obey them.

Paul's epistles were not written, for the most part, to those who knew nothing of Jesus' life, death and resurrection. A certain knowledge of these things is obviously presupposed in Paul's writings. Paul could write, 'The things which you learned and received and heard and saw in me, these do, and the God of peace will be with you' (Phil. 4:9). The Christians at Philippi clearly knew more than what is contained in Paul's Epistle to the Philippians. The same conclusion can be drawn from Paul's Second Epistle to the Thessalonians: 'Therefore, brethren, stand fast and hold the traditions which you were taught, whether by word or our epistle' (2 Thess. 2:15).

## Jesus our example

Although Paul never refers in detail to the life of Jesus, he was much aware of its general tenor. He knew that Christ lived as a poor man (2 Cor. 8:9). So he did: 'Foxes have holes and birds of the air have nests, but the Son of Man has nowhere to lay his head' (Luke 9:58). Paul also referred to 'the meekness and gentleness of Christ' (2 Cor. 10:1) — a sentiment which echoes Christ's call: 'Take my yoke upon you and learn from me, for I am gentle [or meek] and lowly in heart, and you will find rest for your souls' (Matt.11:29).

When calling on Christians to bear with one another, and not divide over minor issues, Paul could point to the example of Christ, that he did not please himself (Rom. 15:3). Hence Christians are to seek to live so as to please and edify others. Christ's earthly existence was that of a servant, humble and obedient in life and death (Phil. 2:7-8). Again, that is a picture which is in harmony with the Gospel presentation of the Lord who serves (Mark 10:35-45; John 13:1-17).

In writing to the churches, Paul assumed that his readers possessed a reasonable knowledge of the life of Christ. Hence Paul urged the Corinthians: 'Imitate me, just as I also imitate Christ' (1 Cor. 11:1). We derive the English word 'mimic' from the Greek word that is translated there as 'imitate'. A similar thought is found in 1 Thessalonians 1:6: 'And you became followers [mimics] of us and of the Lord, having received the word in much affliction, with joy of the Holy Spirit.' If the Corinthian and Thessalonian Christians knew nothing of Jesus' life, Paul's words would have no meaning. Paul assumes more than he needs to reveal about the earthly life of the Master.

### Did Paul ever meet Jesus?

This then raises the question as to whether Paul ever met Jesus personally. When Paul was converted on the road to Damascus, he saw the risen Lord. It is difficult to know exactly what he saw, as he was overwhelmed by a great light and blinded for three days (see Acts 9; 22; 26). Later, however, Paul asked aggressively, 'Have I not seen Jesus Christ our Lord?' (1 Cor. 9:1). He clearly expected the answer to be a resounding 'Yes!' He went on to list some of those who had seen Christ after he had risen bodily from the dead, adding, 'Then last of all he was seen by me also, as by one born out of due time' (1 Cor. 15:8).

But this does not answer the question as to whether Paul had ever laid eyes on Jesus before he rose from the grave. Sometimes 2 Corinthians 5:16 is understood to mean that Paul did in fact do so: 'Therefore, from now on, we regard no one according to the flesh.

Even though we have known Christ according to the flesh, yet now we know him thus no longer.' Johannes Weiss is one who understood the text in this way,[5] whereas Martin Hengel is one who says that Paul 'almost certainly never knew' the Jesus who walked and talked in ancient Judah, Samaria and Galilee.[6]

It is likely that 'according to the flesh' in 2 Corinthians 5:16 refers to the verbs, not to the persons. This would mean that Paul is saying that he once regarded Christ in a wrong and worldly way; indeed, he had hated the person of Jesus Christ. As a Christian, Paul confessed that in the past he had been a blasphemer (1 Tim. 1:13), which can hardly mean that Paul blasphemed the Father for he was a strict Pharisee. Rather, it was Jesus' claims to deity that offended Paul, together with the notion that the cross is all our righteousness before God (note 1 Cor. 1:18-25; Gal. 3:13; Phil. 3:6). But in 2 Corinthians 5 Paul is saying nothing about whether he had actually met Jesus.

Since Paul was raised in Jerusalem (Acts 22:3; 26:4), it is by no means unlikely that he did lay eyes on Jesus at one time or another. Much later, Paul wrote that he was unknown by face to the churches of Judea (Gal. 1:22), and this has been widely interpreted to mean that he could not have spent his pre-Christian youth in Jerusalem. However, Jerusalem had a population of between 10,000 and 150,000 (so varied are the estimates),[7] so it was not the kind of small village where everybody knows everybody else. There is nothing in Galatians 1:22 that contradicts the Acts passages.

But if Paul ever met Christ (it has been suggested, without much supporting evidence, that he was the rich young ruler of Matthew 19), he says nothing about it. In any case, while the Bible lays great emphasis on the hard facts of history (e.g. 1 Cor. 15:3-8), it does not consider that there is any spiritual advantage to be gained by knowing what Jesus looked like (John 20:29; 1 Peter 1:8).

While it cannot be said that Paul makes extensive reference to the life of Christ, it is clear that he did know something of it and assumed a knowledge of it on the part of his converts. We shall see, as our study develops, that there is good reason to go beyond the restraint of this preliminary statement.

# 4.
# Paul's knowledge of Jesus' words

Again we must quote Rudolf Bultmann: 'The teaching of the historical Jesus plays no role, or practically none, in Paul and John.'[1] Only slightly less extreme are the views of S. G. Wilson: 'It is almost impossible to forge significant links between Jesus and Paul on the basis of the sayings of Jesus which appear in the epistles: they are embarrassingly few in number, alluded to rather than quoted, perhaps known only because of their peculiar liturgical or legal status, and above all they are ignored by Paul when it suited his purpose. There is little to encourage links between Jesus and Paul here.'[2] Bultmann and Wilson paint a picture of Paul's evangelism which lacks credibility. There is every indication that Paul knew the words of Christ, and that he expected those in the churches to which he wrote to know them also.

## 1 Corinthians 7:10-11

On a number of occasions, albeit not all that many, Paul specifically cites the words of Jesus. This shows he had access either to some of our Gospels (most scholars reject this possibility, but without much reason) or to material that was later to appear in those Gospels. Writing to the Corinthians on the subject of divorce, Paul declared, 'Now to the married I command, yet not I but the Lord: A wife is not to depart from her husband... And a husband is not to divorce his wife' (1 Cor. 7:10-11). The idea behind this is found in Jesus' words that what God has joined together, man is not to separate (Matt. 19:6; Mark 10:9; Luke 16:18). Clearly, Paul knew Christ's teaching on the subject of divorce and remarriage, and cited its authority rather than his own.

In fact, Paul went on to indicate that he knew very well when he was citing the words of Christ and when he was not. He wrote, 'But to the rest I, not the Lord, say: If any brother has a wife who does not believe, and she is willing to live with him, let him not divorce her' (1 Cor. 7:12). Later he was to add, 'Now concerning virgins: I have no commandment from the Lord; yet I give judgement as one whom the Lord in his mercy has made trustworthy' (1 Cor. 7:25). Those liberal scholars who think that the early churchmen simply made up stories about Jesus to edify their congregations have trouble explaining Paul's careful distinctions between his own words and those of Christ, as set out in 1 Corinthians 7.

David Wenham points out that the context in 1 Corinthians and Matthew 19/Mark 10 shows the strength of the links between the Gospel tradition and Paul.[3] Both refer to the 'one flesh' principle (1 Cor. 6:16; 7:1-5; Matt. 19:4-6) and both refer to the gift of celibacy (1 Cor. 7:7-8; Matt. 19:11-12). It is likely that Paul knew a considerable body of material concerning Jesus' teaching on marriage, divorce and sexual matters.


## 1 Corinthians 9:14 and 1 Timothy 5:18

A second citation occurs in 1 Corinthians 9:14 where Paul states, 'Even so the Lord has commanded that those who preach the gospel should live from the gospel.' A more exact quotation is found in 1 Timothy 5:18: 'The labourer is worthy of his wages.' This is close to Matthew 10:10: 'A worker is worthy of his food,' and identical with Luke 10:7: 'The labourer is worthy of his wages.'

It is interesting that in 1 Corinthians 9 Paul regards Jesus' words as teaching what is just, not what is obligatory. Paul spent a great deal of space in setting out the right of preachers to a stipend (1 Cor.

9:1-14), but then did not make use of that right himself (1 Cor. 9:15-18). It may be that it was the fact that the Corinthians themselves were aware of Jesus' sayings that raised their doubts about Paul: was he really an apostle if he was not being paid a stipend? After all, this man works with his hands, like a common manual labourer (see 1 Cor. 4:12; 9:18; 2 Cor. 11:7; 1 Thess. 2:9). Paul was thus forced to deal with that objection by explaining Christ's words as they applied to himself.

In 1 Timothy 5, however, as Paul writes of elders in the church, he simply says that they are to be financially recompensed. Paul was always more concerned for the rights of others than he was for his own rights.

## 1 Corinthians 11:23-26

In seeking to correct the erratic behaviour of the church at Corinth, Paul reminded his converts of the Last Supper of Christ. His words are familiar to all who remember the Lord's death through fellowship around the Lord's table: 'For I received from the Lord that which I also delivered to you: that the Lord Jesus on the same night in which he was betrayed took bread; and when he had given thanks, he broke it and said, "Take, eat; this is my body which is broken[4] for you; do this in remembrance of me." In the same manner he also took the cup after supper, saying, "This cup is the new covenant in my blood. This do, as often as you drink it, in remembrance of me." For as often as you eat this bread and drink this cup, you proclaim the Lord's death till he comes.'

It was only because the Corinthians were so divided, self-indulgent and unmindful of what Christian fellowship is all about that Paul raised the subject of the Lord's Supper at all. Paul knew details about the Last Supper — for example, he knew that it took place at night — and he saw his teaching as part of a common body of received truth. His words echo Jesus' words in Luke's Gospel which, unlike those in Matthew and Mark, recall the command to 'Do this in remembrance of Me' (Luke 22:19).

Paul's claim concerning his teaching on the supper is that he received it from the Lord and therefore he was delivering it to the church at Corinth (v.23). There was a relay of truth in operation, and its source went back to Christ himself. This may have come by a direct revelation of Christ (as in Gal. 1:11-12) or, perhaps more likely, Paul means that he learnt about the supper from Luke and others, and in turn transmitted this teaching to his own converts. Either way, Paul is revealing that he knew much about Jesus' last night before his crucifixion.

## 1 Thessalonians 4:15-16

In seeking to comfort the Thessalonian Christians who had seen some of their number die, and who had apparently expected to see Christ return before the death of any of them, Paul wrote, 'For this we say to you by the word of the Lord, that we who are alive and remain until the coming of the Lord will by no means precede those who are asleep. For the Lord himself will descend from heaven with a shout, with the voice of an archangel, and with the trumpet of God. And the dead in Christ will rise first' (1 Thess. 4:15-16).

It is possible that the word here was a revelation of Christ received by Paul through the Holy Spirit, but the verses are reminiscent of Jesus' words in Matthew 24:31: 'And he will send his angels with a great sound of a trumpet, and they will gather together his elect from the four winds, from one end of heaven to the other.' Certainly, Paul is claiming Christ's authority for his teaching about the second coming of his Lord.

## Acts 20:35

This is an unusual, but perhaps not unique, case in that it is not immediately obvious that Paul is referring to any saying in the canonical Gospels. In bidding farewell to the elders of the church of Ephesus, Paul spoke of how he had supported himself by working with his own hands. Paul did not conduct his missionary work as a so-called 'faith mission'! Paul went on to say, 'I have shown you in every way, by labouring like this, that you must support the weak. And remember the words of the Lord Jesus, that he said, "It is more blessed to give than to receive"' (Acts 20:35).

The general idea is close to what Jesus says in Luke 6:38: 'Give, and it will be given to you.' But it does seem a little too far from the strict wording of Jesus' injunction for this to be the source of Paul's statement. Towards the end of the first century, about the year A.D. 96, a Christian leader called Clement of Rome wrote to the turbulent church at Corinth reminding them of better days when 'giving was dearer to your hearts than receiving'.[5] This may be a reference to Jesus' words cited in Acts 20:35, but it is more likely that Paul and Clement were both aware of an authentic saying of Jesus which is not found in our Gospels. After all, the last words in the Gospel of John tell us, 'And there are also many other things that Jesus did, which if they were written one by one, I suppose that even the world itself could not contain the books that would be written' (John 21:25).

## Paul's use of the Old Testament

In examining how Paul referred to the words of Jesus, it is instructive to consider briefly how he used the Old Testament. According to E. Earle Ellis, Paul quotes the Old Testament ninety-three times. On fifty-one occasions his citations agree with the Septuagint (the Greek translation of the Old Testament). There are four times when he follows the Hebrew as against the Greek translation, and thirty-eight times when he diverges to some extent from both.[6] It has long been observed that sometimes Paul is quite exact in his quotations, and sometimes he is content simply to give the gist of what the Old Testament says. As Ellis has noted, 'From a psychological viewpoint it might be expected that one who knew the Scripture in several languages and had a thorough knowledge of the sense of Scripture would be less tied to any text-form.'[7]

Paul was no pedant; he viewed direct quotations and free renderings of Scripture as equally valid, if faithfully done. For example, in 1 Corinthians 15:45, Paul states, 'And so it is written, "The first man Adam became a living being." The last Adam became a life-giving spirit.' This is a rather free quotation from Genesis 2:7. If one wished to multiply examples, one could point to 1 Corinthians 1:31, where Paul's 'He who glories, let him glory in the Lord' is obviously a free rendering of Jeremiah 9:23-24; 1 Corinthians 2:9, which seems to be a very free rendering of Isaiah 64:4; 65:17; and 1 Corinthians 15:54-55, which alludes to Isaiah 25:8 and Hosea 13:14, but can hardly be described as strict quotation. Such an approach may explain the difficulty we sometimes have in trying to decide whether Paul is referring to a specific text of Scripture, be it the Old Testament or a record of Jesus' sayings (even some of our Gospels, dare we say it!), or simply alluding to the same. It is grossly misleading to give the impression that Paul only ever referred to Gospel sayings on five or six occasions. There are many allusions, and possible allusions, that also need to be taken into account. This is precisely what one would expect: it is stretching credibility to think that Paul sought to evangelize the highways and byways of the Roman Empire armed only with five or six Gospel sayings.

# 5.
# Echoes of Jesus' words

## 1 Thessalonians 5:21-22

Certainty eludes us yet again, as it did when we looked at Acts 20:35, but there may be another reference by Paul to an unwritten saying of Jesus. Near the end of his First Epistle to the Thessalonians, Paul urged his readers to 'Test all things; hold fast what is good. Abstain from every form of evil' (1 Thess. 5:21-22). In the period of the early church, Clement of Alexandria often quoted this in the form: 'Be ye approved money-changers, who reject much, but retain the good.'[1] With hosts of pilgrims making their way to Jerusalem for the three great feasts of the Passover, Pentecost and Tabernacles, a money-changer needed to keep his wits about him to evaluate the diverse currencies he had to handle. He was always on the lookout for fraudulent coins.

When referring to 1 Thessalonians 5:21-22, the early Christian writers would invariably understand the last part to mean: 'Abstain from every bad sort of money.' Leon Morris is one evangelical scholar who accepts that Paul was probably referring to an authentic saying of Jesus.[2] Just as the money-changer would test each coin to see whether it was the genuine article, so the Christian must test whatever he sees and hears to evaluate whether it is of God or not.

## Romans 12-14

As is well known, the Epistle to the Romans can be divided into two sections — the first eleven chapters dealing with Christian doctrine and the last five chapters dealing with Christian practice. The two sections are joined together by the 'therefore' in Romans 12:1. This is far too simplistic to be totally accurate, but it has enough correspondence with reality to be useful. Of more immediate concern to us is the fact that Paul's treatment of practical Christian living in Romans 12-14 is saturated with the outlook of Christ, especially as set out in the Sermon on the Mount (Matt. 5-7) and the Sermon on the Plain (Luke 6:17-49).

This can easily be demonstrated. Paul wrote, 'Bless those who persecute you; bless and do not curse' (Rom. 12:14). In the Sermon on the Plain, Jesus told his disciples to 'Bless those who curse you, and pray for those who spitefully use you' (Luke 6:28). Paul wrote, 'Repay no one evil for evil' (Rom. 12:17) and 'Do not be overcome by evil, but overcome evil with good' (Rom. 12:21). Such teaching goes back to that of the Master: 'You have heard that it was said, "An eye for an eye and a tooth for a tooth." But I tell you not to resist an evil person. But whoever slaps you on your right cheek, turn the other to him also. If anyone wants to sue you and take away your tunic, let him have your cloak also. And whoever compels you to go one mile, go with him two' (Matt. 5:38-41).

In discussing a Christian's civil responsibilities, Paul told the Roman Christians, 'Render therefore to all their due: taxes to whom taxes are due, customs to whom customs, fear to whom fear, honour to whom honour' (Rom. 13:7). It is not too difficult to see Jesus' teaching behind this, which was given in the context of a question about the correctness of paying taxes to a pagan ruler and summarized in the words, 'Render therefore to Caesar the things that are Caesar's, and to God the things that are God's' (Matt. 22:21).

The injunction to love one's neighbour as oneself (Rom. 13:8-10) also goes back to Christ (Mark 12:31), who cited it from the Old Testament (Lev. 19:18). The laws against adultery, murder, stealing, lying and coveting are not set aside by the command to love, but summed up by it. Love and law go together.

Paul goes on to declare that Christians ought not to judge one another over non-essential matters (Rom. 14:10,13). Christ had also said, 'Judge not, that you be not judged' (Matt. 7:1) — not meaning, as is so often thought today, that nothing can be criticized as being wrong, for Christ spoke of not casting pearls before swine (Matt. 7:6) and of watching out for false prophets (Matt. 7:15-20). Rather, Christ's words are a warning against judging harshly and self-righteously, for we too shall be judged (Matt. 7:2; Rom. 14:10).

Furthermore, Christians are urged not to put a stumbling-block in a brother's way or to cause any fellow Christian to fall (Rom. 14:13). That is why it is good neither to eat meat nor drink wine nor do anything which could cause a brother to stumble or be offended (Rom. 14:20). In a similar vein, the Lord had warned, 'But whoever causes one of these little ones who believe in me to sin, it would be better for him if a millstone were hung around his neck, and he were drowned in the depth of the sea. Woe to the world because of offences! For offences must come, but woe to that man by whom the offence comes!' (Matt. 18:6-7; see also Mark 9:42; Luke 17:1-2; 1 Cor. 8:13). C. E. B. Cranfield writes of the need to recognize the possibility that Paul's teaching may be indebted to Jesus' teaching,[3] but this seems overly cautious. Both Paul and Jesus use the unusual Greek word *'skandalon'* to describe the stumbling-block or the offence, which increases the likelihood that Paul was dependent upon Jesus' teaching. The rabbis used to interpret Leviticus 19:14 in a metaphorical way — about not putting a stumbling-block before the spiritually blind — but Jesus' words still seem to be the most likely source for Paul's words.[4]

A heavy-handed judgement must not be passed on a brother on matters of food or drink because nothing is unclean of itself. But it is also true that to him who considers anything to be unclean, to him it is unclean (Rom. 14:14). Again, it is very probable that Paul had Christ's words in mind: 'There is nothing that enters a man from outside which can defile him; but the things which come out of him, those are the things that defile a man' (Mark 7:15). In saying this, Christ was declaring that all foods were pure (Mark 7:19).

In short, it is clear that Paul's ethical thinking is saturated with that of his divine Master.

## Colossians

The book of Colossians has a number of possible allusions to Jesus'
words, some more obvious than others. When Paul wrote of the
gospel as 'bearing fruit and growing' (Col. 1:6,10, NIV) in the
world, it is by no means unlikely that he had Christ's parable of the
sower in mind, especially the fourth soil. To quote that parable, 'But
other seed fell on good ground and yielded a crop that sprang up,
increased  and produced: some thirtyfold, some sixty, and some a
hundred' (Mark 4:8).

In Colossians 1:13 Paul affirms of God, 'He has delivered us
from the power of darkness and translated us into the kingdom of the
Son of his love.' The description of Christ there matches that given
in the record of his baptism where the Father declared, 'You are my
beloved Son, in whom I am well pleased' (Mark 1:11).

More echoes of the Gospels follow. Paul tells Christians to 'Put
to death your members which are on the earth: fornication, uncleanness, passion, evil desire, and covetousness, which is idolatry' (Col.
3:5). This would appear to be based on Jesus' words that 'If your
hand makes you sin, cut it off' and 'If your foot makes you sin, cut
it off', and 'If your eye makes you sin, pluck it out' (Mark 9:43,
45,47). There is good reason to believe that Paul knew what we call
the Lord's Prayer. Paul exhorts us to bear with one another, forgive
one another, if anyone has a complaint against another; even as
Christ has forgiven us, so we must also (Col. 3:13; see also Eph.
4:32). The way that Paul connects God's forgiveness of us with our
forgiveness of other Christians is very reminiscent of Jesus' teaching: 'Forgive us our debts, as we also have forgiven our debtors'
(Matt. 6:12, NIV; see also Luke 11:4).

The emphasis on watching and praying is found both in Paul and
in Jesus (Col. 4:2; Mark 14:38). Finally, Paul's call to Christians for
our speech always to be with grace, 'seasoned with salt' (Col. 4:6)
surely harks back to Jesus' teaching: 'Have salt in yourselves, and
have peace with one another' (Mark 9:50).

## 1 Thessalonians 5

Another cluster of allusions to Jesus' words can be found in 1 Thessalonians 5. Paul writes confidently to the church of Thessalonica, 'For you yourselves know perfectly that the day of the Lord so comes as a thief in the night' (1 Thess. 5:2). This reminds us of Luke 12:39-40: 'But know this, that if the master of the house had known what hour the thief would come, he would have watched and not allowed his house to be broken into. Therefore you also be ready, for the Son of Man is coming at an hour you do not expect.' The point is that not only is Paul familiar with Jesus' words, but he expects the Thessalonian Christians to be familiar with them too. In fact, Paul had even written that 'Concerning the times and the seasons, brethren, you have no need that I should write to you' (1 Thess. 5:1). In addition, it is surely obvious that Paul would not have been the originator of the startling, and even somewhat unseemly, picture of Christ as a thief in the night. Such a picture must go back to Christ himself. We can only conclude that the knowledge of Jesus' teachings concerning the Second Coming was evidently widespread.

The call to watch and be sober, in the light of Christ's second coming, is found both in 1 Thessalonians 5:4-7 and Matthew 24:42-50. The command for Christians to be at peace among themselves is also found in 1 Thessalonians 5:13 and Mark 9:50. Paul went on to say, 'See that no one renders evil for evil to anyone, but always pursue what is good both for yourselves and for all' (1 Thess. 5:15). This is an obvious echo of Jesus' teaching in the Sermon on the Mount (Matt. 5:38-48; see also Luke 6:27-36). The call to 'Pray without ceasing' (1 Thess. 5:17) echoes the message of the parable of the persistent widow, which is designed to encourage us always to pray and not to lose heart (Luke 18:1-8).

## Many other echoes

Throughout Paul's epistles there are numerous other echoes and possible echoes of Jesus' words. To the church in Rome, which was

mainly Gentile rather than Jewish (cf. Rom. 11:16-24), Paul nevertheless used an Aramaic word, *'Abba'*, in describing the Christian's
attitude to his heavenly Father. Paul wrote, 'For you did not receive
the spirit of bondage again to fear, but you received the Spirit of
adoption by whom we cry out, "Abba, Father"' (Rom. 8:15; see too
Gal. 4:6).

How did Paul come to address the High and Holy One with such
familial affection? It was Christ who taught his disciples to call upon
God as 'Our Father in heaven' (Matt. 6:9). In the agony of
Gethsemane, he himself prayed, 'Abba, Father, all things are
possible for you. Take this cup away from me; nevertheless, not
what I will, but what you will' (Mark 14:36). It does not require a
vivid imagination nor an obscurantist outlook to maintain that the
most obvious explanation for Paul's 'Abba' references is that they
go back ultimately to Christ himself.

Paul's call to the Roman Christians to be wise in what is good,
and simple (or innocent) in what is evil (Rom. 16:19; see also 1 Cor.
14:20) is surely more than 'a little reminiscent' — which is all that
C. E. B. Cranfield will allow[5] — of Jesus' words in Matthew 10:16.
Similarly, when Paul wrote that 'It is required in stewards that one
be found faithful' (1 Cor. 4:2), he may well have had Jesus' words
in mind: 'Who then is that faithful and wise steward, whom his
master will make ruler over his household, to give him his portion
of food in due season?' (Luke 12:42, slightly altered). Christ also
declared that 'No servant can serve two masters' (Luke 16:13), and
teaching of this kind must form the background to Paul's stark
presentation of the same thought in Romans 6:16.

When the Lord Jesus sent out the seventy (or seventy-two) on a
mission of preaching and healing, he told them, 'Whatever city you
enter, and they receive you, eat such things as are set before you'
(Luke 10:8). Gentiles might have offered them food that was
unclean (not *kosher*) according to the laws set out in Leviticus 11.
Later, Paul had trouble with the church at Corinth where Christians
were debating whether they could rightfully eat meat that might
have been offered to idols. Paul's words are reminiscent of Christ's:

'Eat whatever is set before you' (1 Cor. 10:27). The two situations were not identical, but the same principles were applicable to both. Paul appears to be drawing upon his knowledge of what Christ had said in Luke 10.

In contemplating the future life of the believer in Christ, Paul affirmed, 'For we know that if our earthly house, this tent, is destroyed, we have a building from God, a house not made with hands, eternal in the heavens' (2 Cor. 5:1). There has been some debate as to whether the 'house not made with hands' is a house in heaven (as Charles Hodge thinks[6]) or the resurrection body (as Philip Edgcumbe Hughes thinks[7]). If Hodge is correct, it is possible that behind Paul's words of comfort were Jesus' words in John 14:2: 'In my Father's house are many mansions; if it were not so, I would have told you. I go to prepare a place for you.' However, Hughes' view seems the more likely, and this raises the issue as to whether Paul knew of Jesus' saying reported at his trial, 'I will destroy this temple that is made with hands, and within three days I will build another made without hands' (Mark 14:58; note John 2:19-21). Hughes goes so far as to assert that 'Paul's terminology here makes it virtually certain that the Apostle had this dominical saying in mind when he was writing these words.'[8]

A revealing episode is uncovered in the Corinthian correspondence where Paul was on the defensive, trying to explain why he had not come to Corinth when he had declared his intention to do so. He wrote, 'Therefore, when I was planning this, did I do it lightly? Or the things I plan, do I plan according to the flesh, that with me there should be Yes, Yes, and No, No? But as God is faithful, our word to you was not Yes and No' (2 Cor. 1:17-18). It does not require a vivid imagination to postulate that both Paul and the Corinthians were aware of the teaching of Matthew 5:37. It also seems rather likely that there is a connection between Paul's comment that if the rulers of this age had known the Lord of glory they would not have crucified him (1 Cor. 2:8) and Christ's cry of forgiveness from the cross: 'Father, forgive them, for they do not know what they do' (Luke 23:34).

**Similar imagery**

The image of the dead in Christ being asleep is used by our Lord
(Luke 8:52; John 11:11,13), and is found too in Paul's writings (1 Cor.
15:51; 1 Thess. 4:14-15). The image can be traced back to Daniel
12:2, but there it is used to describe all who are in their graves,
whether saved or damned. Hence it seems that Paul's use of the
image is based on that of Jesus, not Daniel.

There is a rather odd image used by Paul as he wrote to the
exuberant Corinthians, who tended to overvalue the more spectacu-
lar gifts in the church and undervalue what is more lasting and
worthwhile. Paul reminded them of their unity in the Spirit: 'For by
one Spirit we were all baptized into one body — whether Jews or
Greeks, whether slaves or free — and have all been made to drink
of one Spirit' (1 Cor. 12:13, slightly altered). All Christians have
been baptized in the Spirit; it is not a second work of grace but
another way of expressing what conversion means. The reference to
'drinking of one Spirit', or 'drinking the Spirit', seems to be only
another way of saying the same thing. But it an unusual expression,
and may well go back to Jesus' words recorded in John's Gospel.
Jesus told the Samaritan woman by the well at Sychar: 'Whoever
drinks of this water will thirst again, but whoever drinks of the water
that I shall give him will never thirst. But the water that I shall give
him will become in him a fountain of water springing up into
everlasting life' (John 4:13-14). Later, at the Feast of Tabernacles,
he cried out to the crowd: 'If anyone thirsts, let him come to me and
drink. He who believes in me, as the Scripture has said, out of his
heart will flow rivers of living water.' John himself then explains:
'But this he spoke concerning the Spirit, whom those believing in
him would receive; for the Holy Spirit was not yet given, because
Jesus was not yet glorified' (John 7:37-39). It is difficult to explain
Paul's metaphor without recourse to the words of Jesus.

As our Lord encouraged his disciples to persevere in the task of
evangelism, he stated, 'And he who reaps receives wages, and
gathers fruit for eternal life, that both he who sows and he who reaps
may rejoice together. For in this the saying is true: "One sows and

another reaps." I sent you to reap that for which you have not laboured; others have laboured, and you have entered into their labours' (John 4:36-38). Paul picks up the same image, and essentially the same message, in 1 Corinthians 3 where he speaks of himself as planting, Apollos as watering and God as giving the increase (1 Cor. 3:6-9). It is, of course, impossible to prove that Paul had Jesus' words in mind.

A similar impossibility is found in Romans 6:19 where Paul writes, 'I speak in human terms because of the weakness of your flesh. For just as you presented your members as slaves of uncleanness, and of lawlessness leading to more lawlessness, so now present your members as slaves of righteousness for holiness.' Dr Martyn Lloyd-Jones never liked to think that Paul was apologizing for the slavery analogy that he was using.[9] But it is not altogether unlikely that Paul was somewhat hesitant about referring to Christians as slaves because of what Jesus said in John 15:15, 'No longer do I call you servants, for a servant does not know what his master is doing; but I have called you friends, for all things that I heard from My Father I have made known to you.'

We need to be careful of claiming too much. It was not for nothing that Samuel Sandmel once complained of 'parallelomania', which he defined as 'that extravagance among scholars which first overdoes the supposed similarity in passages and then proceeds to describe source and derivation as if implying literary connection flowing in an inevitable or predetermined direction'.[10] However, it is interesting, to put it no more strongly, that Paul and Jesus so often use similar imagery.

The great apostle and his Lord both use illustrations such as a grain of wheat (1 Cor. 15:36-37; John 12:24), sowing (1 Cor. 3:6; 2 Cor. 9:10; Mark 4:1-20,26-27), building (1 Cor. 3:10-11; Matt. 7:24) and treasure (2 Cor. 4:7; Matt. 13:44). When Paul declares of the Corinthian Christians, 'I have betrothed you to one husband, that I may present you as a chaste virgin to Christ' (2 Cor. 11:2), it is more than possible that he had in mind Jesus' parable of the wise and foolish virgins (Matt. 25:1-13). Immoral behaviour and false teaching are portrayed by Paul as a leaven that operates within the whole lump (1 Cor. 5:6-7; Gal. 5:9). This reminds us of Jesus' warning: 'Take heed and beware of the leaven of the Pharisees and the Sadducees' (Matt. 16:6). The leaven imagery is also used in a favourable way, to describe the expansion of the kingdom of heaven in Matthew 13:33.

Like Jesus (Mark 11:23; Matt. 17:20), Paul linked faith with the moving of mountains (1 Cor. 13:2). Sometimes this is said to be a proverbial Jewish phrase from which both men draw, but the connection with faith is not attested in the rabbinic sayings.[11] Furthermore, Paul sets out the principle that 'Whatever a man sows, that he will also reap' (Gal. 6:7; see also 2 Cor. 9:6). This echoes Jesus' parable where the wicked and useless servant tries to justify his hiding the Lord's money in a handkerchief by saying, 'For I feared you, because you are an austere man. You collect what you did not deposit, and reap what you did not sow' (Luke 19:21). But the image is also found in the Old Testament (Prov. 22:8; Hosea 10:12-13). For that matter, the saying can be found in the writings of Antiphon on education in ancient Athens: 'As one sows, so can one expect to reap.'[12]

The same can be said of the 'light' imagery. Christians are said to be 'light in the Lord', and so they are to 'walk as children of light' (Eph. 5:8). As Paul told the Thessalonians, 'You are all sons of light and sons of the day' (1 Thess. 5:5). 'Light' is a rather obvious image to use in matters of religion. The psalmist describes the Lord as his light (Ps. 27:1) and pleads that God would send out his light and his truth (Ps. 43:3). In anticipation of Messianic blessings, the Gentiles are exhorted, 'Arise, shine; for your light has come' (Isa. 60:1). The Lord himself would be their everlasting light (Isa. 60:19-20). But it may well be that Paul had in mind Jesus' words to his disciples: 'You are the light of the world' (Matt. 5:14). Christ went on to say, 'I am the light of the world. He who follows Me shall not walk in darkness, but have the light of life' (John 8:12). The unbeliever loves the darkness, but the believer repents of sin, does the truth and comes to the light (John 3:19-21).

Both Paul and Jesus warn against following 'blind guides' (Matt. 15:14; 23:16; Rom. 2:19); both speak of weighing up the gains and losses involved in following Christ (Mark 8:35-37; Phil. 3:7); both are critical of those who seek after signs (Matt. 12:38-39; 16:1-4; John 4:48; 1 Cor.1:22-23); both tell of the condemned sinner being speechless at the judgement (Matt. 22:12; Rom. 3:19); both link faith with not being worried about worldly concerns (Matt. 6:25-34; Phil. 4:6-7); and both warn that should a person deny Christ in this life, he in turn will be denied before the Father at the judgement (Matt. 10:33; 2 Tim. 2:12).

The use of similar images, similar words and similar concepts does not in itself prove that Paul was dependent upon the words of Jesus, transmitted either in oral or written form. But it does point to a certain harmony between the two. The widespread assumption in some scholars that every hint of connection and harmony needs to be explained away is out of touch with reality. In the writings of Paul, there are many echoes of the words of Jesus. Arnold Resch in 1904 went overboard when he asserted that he had discovered 925 allusions to Jesus' teachings in what he thought were the nine Pauline letters, another 133 in Ephesians, 100 in the Pastoral Epistles, sixty-four in Paul's speeches in Acts, and dozens of here-tofore unknown sayings of Jesus in Paul's letters.[13] We must content ourselves in the knowledge that Paul knew much of the Gospel record of Jesus. Indeed, he may have known all of it plus some extra authentic sayings and accounts that have since been lost.

# 6.
# The basic gospel in Paul and Jesus

It can be clearly shown that Paul and Jesus possessed a common understanding of the fallen human condition, and of the need to repent and to trust Christ on the basis of his glorious person and work in order to be received by God.

## The human condition

The older liberals tended to be quite optimistic about human nature; they believed in progress, the inevitability of evolution, Western civilization, cultural achievements and the perfectability of mankind. This affected the way they read the Scriptures. F. G. Bratton, to cite one such liberal, referred to 'Jesus' supreme faith in the goodness of humanity'.[1] Not many now would want to endorse that statement without qualification, but the old liberal melody manages to linger on, sometimes in what might seem to be unexpected places. The Roman Catholic Church today is capitulating to theological liberalism just when liberalism has revealed its own spiritual and moral bankruptcy. Hence the Roman priest Wilfrid Harrington declares of Jesus: 'He took his stand on the Fatherhood (Motherhood) of God.' In addition, 'He firmly believed that all men and women are children of the Father/Mother, that all are brothers and sisters.'[2] Such a view implies that human beings are not too offensive to the holy majesty of God. Prevailing scholarly opinion is that, in comparison with Jesus, 'It is clear that Paul works with a more pessimistic view of human nature and indeed of creation as a whole.'[3]

What is abundantly clear is that Paul possessed no rosy-eyed view of the human condition. Sin is everywhere, as can be shown by human experience (Rom. 1:18-32) and by Scripture (Rom. 3:10-20). The world is referred to as 'this present evil age' (Gal. 1:4). Christians are made alive in Christ, but their starting-point is sad indeed: they were dead in trespasses and sins; they pursued the lusts and desires of the flesh and the mind and they were by nature children of wrath, just as non-Christians are (Eph. 2:1-3). This corruption has been inherited from Adam (Rom. 5:12-21).

The natural man, i.e. man as he is in his fallen condition, apart from the special grace of the Holy Spirit, is hostile to God, unable to obey God's law, and unable to please God (Rom. 8:7-8). Far from reaching out for God, the unbeliever is alienated from him (Col. 1:21). The natural condition of human beings is painted in bleak colours — their minds are futile, their understanding darkened, their hearts hardened, and they are given over to sin (Eph. 4:17-24).

This is not to say that unbelievers are not able to do some good in a limited sense (e.g. Rom. 13:3-4), nor that their judgements are without value (see 2 Cor. 8:21; 1 Tim. 3:7). But sin has such a powerful hold over humanity that even the Christian, forgiven in Christ and indwelt by the Holy Spirit, is engaged in a constant battle within himself (Rom. 7:14-25; Gal. 5:17). How often do we do that which we hate and not do the good that we intend to do!

But is Paul's view of the human condition any more depressing than that of Jesus himself? It seems that our Lord never taught that human beings were so close to God that they only required a little polish and they would be acceptable before him who is thrice holy and who inhabits eternity. Jesus began his ministry with the general call to 'Repent, for the kingdom of heaven is at hand' (Matt. 4:17). He went on to assert, 'I tell you, no; but unless you repent you will all likewise perish' (Luke 13:3,5). Such a call presupposes that all humanity is weighed down by sin. It is not enough for the fruit to be good; the whole tree has to be made good (Matt. 12:33-34).

As Jesus taught his disciples about prayer, he declared, 'If you then, being evil, know how to give good gifts to your children, how much more will your heavenly Father give the Holy Spirit to those who ask him!' (Luke 11:13). Even when we do good things — like looking after our children — our nature is still evil. Such is the purity of God that only he can be called 'good' (Matt. 19:17). One may keep all the commandments in an outward sense, and still be lacking in God's sight (Matt. 19:16-22).

Even when people witnessed Jesus' miracles and believed in his name, our Lord was wary. The apostle John tells us, 'Jesus did not commit himself to them, because he knew all men, and had no need that anyone should testify of man, for he knew what was in man' (John 2:24-25). Further on, Christ declares, 'And this is the condemnation, that the light has come into the world, and men loved darkness rather than light, because their deeds were evil' (John 3:19). Our natural spiritual condition can only be described as a kind of bondage which requires the Son to set us free (John 8:32-36) or a kind of death which requires the Son to give us life (John 5:24-25). Sin is not something that lies on the surface of our being: 'For out of the heart proceed evil thoughts, murders, adulteries, fornications, thefts, false witness, blasphemies' (Matt. 15:19). It is our hearts that defile us.

Both Paul and Jesus taught that we are by nature bound in sin. Not even intense religious zeal or marvellous feats of missionary endeavour can save us. The Pharisees travelled land and sea to win one proselyte, but only succeeded in making him twice as much a son of hell as they were themselves (Matt. 23:15). Those who thought they were offering God service would be found among the most bitter opponents of the early Christians (John 16:2). Zeal for God is an admirable thing, but only if it is allied to knowledge (Rom. 10:2). We human beings, even if we are devout human beings, are utterly unable to bring ourselves to God in a fit condition for him to approve of us.

**The person of Christ**

Modern unbelieving scholars have finely tuned the ancient art of denying the obvious. Wilfrid Harrington, for example, writes, without apparent embarrassment, that 'Paul does not have a christology of pre-existence and incarnation.'⁴ In fact, even a cursory reading of Paul's letters indicates that he viewed Jesus as the divine Redeemer. Christ was in the form of God in heaven but emptied himself of the trappings of glory in order to take upon himself servanthood to the point of death on a cross. Therefore, he was exalted again to heaven, and given the name which is above every name, that all should bow to him and confess that he is Lord (Phil. 2:6-11).

Christ was present with the ancient Israelites as they made their way from Egypt into the promised land during the fifteenth century B.C. (1 Cor. 10:4). When the time had fully come, in order to save sinners, whose sin meant they could not be saved by the law, God sent his Son (Rom. 8:3; Gal. 4:4). He was revealed in the flesh (1 Tim. 3:16), having left the riches of glory to take on our poverty, that we might be made rich through him (2 Cor. 8:9). Because of his high estimation of Jesus' person, Paul prayed three times to the Lord Jesus to take away his thorn in the flesh (2 Cor. 12:7-9).

The very title of 'God' was applied to Jesus by the great apostle. Paul looked forward to the glorious appearing of 'our great God and Saviour Jesus Christ' (Titus 2:13). Some English translations do their best to hide the fact, but by far the more likely rendering in Romans 9:5 is that 'Christ came, who is over all, the eternally blessed God.' This balances the sentence, as Paul had been saying that in his humanity ('according to the flesh') the Messiah was an Israelite by race.

To Paul, Christ can only be described as 'the Lord of glory' (1 Cor. 2:8). 'He is the image of the invisible God, the firstborn over all creation,' says Colossians 1:15, which fits in with Jesus' claim that those who have seen him have seen the Father (John 14:9). Paul goes on to write of Christ, 'For by him all things were created that are in heaven and that are on earth, visible and invisible, whether thrones or dominions or principalities or powers. All things were created through him and for him. And he is before all things, and in him all things consist' (Col. 1:16-17). Jesus Christ is the agent of creation and the new creation, and hence has the pre-eminence in all things (Col. 1:18).

Paul used the word 'Lord' something like 275 times in his writings, the vast majority of which were references to the lordship of Jesus (e.g. Rom. 10:9). Here, Paul was obviously not simply paying his respect to a venerable personality, but bowing in adoration before the one in whom 'dwells all the fulness of the Godhead bodily' (Col. 2:9). Of Christ, Paul can write, 'He who descended is also the one who ascended far above all the heavens, that he might fill all things' (Eph. 4:10). Christ himself had claimed the capacity to be everywhere at the same time (Matt. 18:20; 28:20), and Paul was only drawing out the full implications of what that meant.

Unbelievers persist in portraying Jesus as a wandering Galilean peasant who somehow became mistaken for God. Charles Raven asserted, 'Jesus is not shown to us as the divine intruder.'[5] More recently, Barbara Thiering has written of *Jesus the Man*[6] — but the result is a work riddled with as much lunacy as heresy.

Often it is acknowledged that the Jesus of John's Gospel is a divine person — which is why so many think John's Gospel is unreliable. Jesus is the Word who was with God and who was God (John 1:1). Wilhelm Wrede asserted dogmatically that 'Intimate disciples could not so readily believe that the man with whom they had sat at table in Capernaum, or sailed on the Lake of Galilee, was the creator of the world.'[7] But John had no such trouble. He wrote, as Paul did in Colossians 1:15, that 'All things were made through him, and without him nothing was made that was made' (John 1:3). Christ made the world, yet the world did not know him (John 1:10). He is 'the only begotten God', as the New American Standard Version rightly has it, who has made known or explained the Father (John 1:18).

Christ presents himself as the eternal one, the incarnation of the 'I AM' who appeared in the burning bush to Moses (Exod. 3:1-14). He claimed that Abraham had seen his day and was glad — an

assertion which confused many of his hearers (John 8:56-57). He
then went on to make an even more astounding claim: 'Most
assuredly, I say to you, before Abraham was, I AM' (John 8:58). The
Jews did not believe what he was saying, but they did at least
understand it, so they picked up stones to stone him for blasphemy
(John 8:59). Jesus, as the Son of God, is equal to his Father (John
5:18). Hence, Christ can make the stupendous claim that he has the
capacity to grant eternal life to sinners who trust in him (John 10:28).
It is small wonder that when Thomas came to understand who Jesus
is, he confessed him as 'my Lord and my God' (John 20:28).

But the Jesus of the Synoptic Gospels is no different. Whereas
the Old Testament repeatedly calls for faith in God, the New
Testament repeatedly does likewise for Christ. Christ commended
those who had great faith in him (Matt. 8:10; 15:28). He declared the
forgiveness of sins for one who trusted in him (Mark 2:5). He told
Jairus, whose daughter had just died, not to be afraid but to believe
(Mark 5:36). It was faith in Christ that made blind Bartimæus well
(Mark 10:52).

Jesus functions as God — he forgives sins in a way that would
be blasphemous were he not God in the flesh (Mark 2:1-12); he
raises the dead (Luke 7:11-17; 8:40-56; see also John 11); and he
will determine the eternal destiny of every human being who has
ever lived (Matt. 25:32). He never portrayed himself as only another
prophet, but as one who is greater than Jonah and Solomon (Matt.
12:41-42). When people responded to Christ, they did not simply
admire and obey him; they worshipped him (Matt. 2:11; 8:2;
9:18;14:33; 15:25; 20:20; 28:9,17; Luke 24:51-52).

Jesus called himself David's Son and David's Lord (Matt. 22:41-
46). This confused the Pharisees who were so hostile to him that they
did not want to understand what he said. But as a man descended
from the line of David, Jesus is the Son of David; and as God who
reigns in heaven, Jesus is the Lord of David. Wilhelm Bousset tried
to convince people that the early Jewish Christians did not worship
Jesus as Lord.[8] He thought that Paul and the Hellenistic Christians
were the first to invent that title. But Jesus told his disciples that he
would judge the world as Lord of all (Matt. 7:21-23; see also Matt.

22:44-46; Mark 11:3; John 13:13-14). It is precisely because he is Lord that we ought to do what he says (Luke 6:46). So common was it for the early Christians, whether Jews or Hellenists, to refer to Jesus as Lord that Paul used the Aramaic word *'Maranatha'*, meaning, 'O Lord, come', when writing to a Greek church (1 Cor. 16:22). The word must have been so well used that Greek Christians understood it even though it was an Aramaic word.

The Jesus who is presented to us in Paul's epistles is the same Jesus who is presented to us in the Gospels, whether in the Synoptics or in John.

## The death of Jesus

There are people who think that Paul saw Jesus as a redeemer from sin, but that Jesus saw himself as a teacher from God. They then blame Paul for placing so much emphasis on the death of our Lord Jesus Christ. This view is put forward by Wilhelm Bousset[9] and Wilhelm Wrede.[10] Johannes Weiss also thought that Jesus and Paul were poles apart on the subject of redemption: 'The difference remains between the voluntary and immediate apprehension of God's love in childlike confidence, and the belief that man may venture to approach God, because God Himself has offered the necessary sacrifice upon the Cross of Christ.'[11] At times there seems no end to the misunderstanding achieved by scholars. Wilfrid Harrington writes of Christ's death: 'His death set humankind free because his life was laid down in defence of the value and dignity of the human person.'[12] He goes on to claim that any idea of Christ's paying the penalty for sin is 'a travesty of the gospel' and 'a caricature of God'.[13]

It is surely clear enough that Paul saw Christ's death as an act of redemption and atonement. At the cross, Christ was set forth as a propitiation whereby the righteous justice and holy anger of God was satisfied (Rom. 3:25). The Sinless One was made to be sin by a gracious act of substitution (2 Cor. 5:21). As sinners, we are all under the curse of not having completely obeyed everything that is written in the book of God's law (Gal. 3:10). But the good news for the believer is that 'Christ has redeemed us from the curse of the law, having become a curse for us' (Gal. 3:13). Christ's death is an offering and a sacrifice to God (Eph. 5:2); it is what brings peace between God and the penitent sinner (Col. 1:20). Christ gave himself as a ransom (1 Tim. 2:6), that 'He might redeem us from every lawless deed and purify for himself his own special people, zealous for good works' (Titus 2:14).

How did Jesus view his own death? To cite the hapless Harrington again: 'Jesus began his mission with optimism. He did not start off with a grim vision of a violent death at the end of the road.'[14] Not so at all. In John's Gospel, John the Baptist proclaimed the Messiah as 'the Lamb of God who takes away the sin of the world', and Jesus never uttered a word of contradiction (John 1:29, see also v. 36). This description obviously points back to the Old Testament sacrifices where the death of an animal was accepted in place of that of the sinner. As Leon Morris says of Christ, 'He is the complete embodiment of all the truth to which the sacrificial system pointed.'[15]

In speaking to Nicodemus, Jesus points to his death: 'And as Moses lifted up the serpent in the wilderness, even so must the Son of Man be lifted up, that whoever believes in him should not perish but have eternal life' (John 3:14-15, referring to events described in Num. 21:4-9). Christ is here prefigured by a bronze serpent, not a lamb; by a symbol of evil, not of innocence. Since the Lord Jesus is the Sinless One (John 8:29,46; 14:30; 15:10), this typology is only appropriate because of Christ's act of substitution. On the cross, Christ was bearing the sins of his people.

The Lord is also portrayed as the Good Shepherd who gives his life for the sheep (John 10:11), meaning that he has died in their place. After the raising of Lazarus from the dead, Caiaphas, the high priest, declared that it was better that one man should die for the people rather than that the whole nation should perish (John 11:49-50). The Gospel writer then explains: 'Now this he did not say on his own authority; but being high priest that year he prophesied that Jesus would die for the nation, and not for that nation only, but also that he would gather together in one the children of God who were scattered abroad' (John 11:51-52). Christ's death was substitutionary, but not in the sense that Caiaphas meant it. The self-serving high priest, like Balaam of old, preached the truth unwittingly.

In the Synoptic Gospels too there is ample evidence that Jesus saw his coming death as an act of redemption, not simply as one that would inspire admiration. Our Lord prophesied his own death and resurrection on a number of occasions (Mark 8:31-33; 9:30-32; 10:32-34) — not that there is any scope in the closed liberal view of life for anything as supernatural as prophecy. Jesus affirmed that he had come as the Son of Man to give his life a ransom for (or 'instead of') many (Mark 10:45). In the Old Testament, a ransom was used to designate a life that would otherwise be forfeit (Exod. 21:30), the money paid for the release of a captive (Lev. 25:51-52) or the equivalent accepted instead of certain sacrifices (Num. 18:15). The death of the Suffering Servant would justify many (Isa. 53) — a notion which forms the background to the utterance of Jesus.

At the Last Supper, Christ took the bread, blessed and broke it, and gave it to the disciples, saying, 'Take, eat; this my body' (Matt. 26:26). He spoke of his blood being shed for many for the remission of sins (Matt. 26:28). In fact, all four Gospels lay much emphasis on the record of Christ's death, and the events leading up to it (see Matt. 21-27; Mark 11-15; Luke 9:51; 19:28 - 23:56; John 12-19). It is inconceivable that Paul was responsible for dreaming up the idea of substitutionary atonement; it is found in the teachings of Christ himself.

## Jesus' resurrection and second coming

The resurrection of Jesus is seen by Paul as the centre of the Christian hope — it is that which declares Jesus to be the Son of God with power (Rom. 1:4) and which gives meaning and direction to the Christian (1 Cor. 15:19). Christ's resurrection brings new life to his people — a new life that begins here and now (Rom. 6:4-10; 8:11-13). To Paul, the resurrection of Christ from the dead is: an authentic and well-authenticated historical event (1 Cor. 15:1-11); the lynchpin of the whole Christian edifice (1 Cor. 15:12-19, 29-34); the defeat of the consequences of the fall of Adam (1 Cor. 15:20-28); the investing of the body with spiritual qualities (1 Cor. 15:35-49); and the pointer to the final and complete victory to come (1 Cor. 15:50-58). Heresy on such a crucial issue warrants firm disciplinary action by the church (1 Tim. 1:20; 2 Tim. 2:17-18). David Jenkins, the former Bishop of Durham, with his flippant remark about the resurrection being 'a conjuring trick with bones', belongs with Hymenaeus and Philetus, not with Paul.

Christ's resurrection means that, for the Christian, 'to die is gain' (Phil. 1:21). Its truth is to dominate the thoughts of the believer. Paul sought to know Christ 'and the power of his resurrection, and the fellowship of his sufferings, being conformed to his death, if, by any means, I may attain to the resurrection from the dead' (Phil. 3:10-11). The Lord Jesus had comforted his disciples: 'Because I live, you will live also' (John 14:19). The full meaning of this is drawn out by the apostle Paul: 'For our citizenship is in heaven, from which we also eagerly wait for the Saviour, the Lord Jesus Christ, who will transform our lowly body that it may be conformed to his glorious body, according to the working by which he is able even to subdue all things to himself' (Phil. 3:20-21).

The Christ who is now enthroned in glory will come again, to usher in the last judgement and, for the believer, the final defeat of death. The prospect of this will motivate the Christian in his battle with sin (Rom. 13:11-13; 1 Thess. 5:2-8) and comfort him in his affliction (Rom. 8:18). Some scholars think that Paul expected to be still alive when Christ returned because he told the Thessalonians that 'We who are alive and remain until the coming of the Lord will by no means precede those who are asleep' (1 Thess. 4:15; see also the 'we' in 1 Cor. 15:51). But Paul obviously used 'we' in a very general sense, meaning 'we Christians, whoever they be'. In 2 Corinthians 5:1 Paul writes, 'For we know that if our earthly house, this tent, is destroyed, we have a building from God, a house not made with hands, eternal in the heavens.' Paul could identify both with those who might still be living at the time of Christ's second coming and with those who might have already died. Later, Paul realized that he was certainly going to belong to the latter group (2 Tim. 4:6).

Paul always expected some kind of interval to elapse between the ascension of our Lord and his return. The gospel had to go out to the nations (Rom. 15:14-33; 1 Tim. 3:16), the full complement of the predestined elect of the Gentiles had to be brought into the fold (Rom. 11) and the man of sin had to appear with an attendant apostasy from the truth (2 Thess. 2:1-12). Then all things would be made right, 'when the Lord Jesus is revealed from heaven with his mighty angels, in flaming fire taking vengeance on those who do not know God, and on those who do not obey the gospel of our Lord Jesus Christ. These shall be punished with everlasting destruction from the presence of the Lord and from the glory of his power, when he comes, in that Day, to be glorified in his saints and to be admired [or "marvelled at" as the NIV puts it] among all those who believe, because our testimony among you was believed' (2 Thess. 1:7-10).

Paul's teachings regarding the resurrection and Second Coming of Christ are based squarely on the teachings of the Lord himself. The unbelieving Sadducees tried to repudiate the idea of a resurrection by postulating a rather absurd example of a woman having seven successive husbands, all brothers, and then asking whose wife she would be in the resurrection. But Christ replied that they did not know the Scriptures nor the power of God. There is no marriage in the resurrection, but, more importantly, once God has established a saving relationship with his people, that relationship remains for all eternity. He is not the God of the dead, but of the living (Matt. 22:23-32).

The Lord prophesied his own death and resurrection, both in the Synoptic Gospels (Mark 8:31-32; 9:30-32; 10:32-34) and in the Gospel of John (John 2:19-21; 10:17-18). Many of Jesus' parables tell of his departure from this earth and his return after a time. The parable of the minas was specifically told because many of Christ's hearers thought that the kingdom of God would appear immediately (Luke 19:11, then vv.12-27). In the parable of the wise and foolish virgins, the return of the bridegroom is delayed, and when he does arrive, he finds five of the virgins unprepared for him (Matt. 25:1-

13). A similar message is found in the parable of the talents (Matt. 25:14-30) and the parable of the sheep and the goats (Matt. 25:31-46). In returning to heaven, Christ was going to prepare a place for his people: 'And if I go and prepare a place for you, I will come again and receive you to myself; that where I am, there you may be also' (John 14:3).

Again, it is clear that no wedge can be driven between Paul and Jesus regarding Christ's rising from the dead and his coming again in glory.

## The Holy Spirit

A. M. Hunter, a biblical scholar who has more regard for the reliability of the Bible than most, still writes of Paul that 'It would be straining the evidence to say he regarded the Spirit as a divine person.'[16] In fact, both Paul and Jesus teach that the Holy Spirit is a divine person. Just after his resurrection, Jesus told his disciples to go into all the world and teach whatever he had taught them. They were to baptize those who turned to Christ in the name of the Father, Son and Holy Spirit (Matt. 28:19-20). The one name, which is the divine name, covers the three persons — the Father, the Son and the Holy Spirit.

Such a view of the Spirit of God is found in the Gospels and the Pauline epistles (as well as the rest of the New Testament). Jesus teaches that the Spirit is a person, not just a force or influence. The Spirit teaches (Luke 12:12; John 14:26) and speaks (John 16:13); he inspired the Old Testament saints (Matt. 22:43) and would inspire the New Testament saints (John 14:26). Furthermore, as a divine person, he can be blasphemed (Matt. 12:31).

The Spirit is a 'he', not an 'it' (e.g. John 16:13-14). His main task is to glorify Christ by taking what is his and declaring it to his people (John 16:14-15). This is precisely what Paul teaches. Sad indeed is the condition of the natural man, the man without the Holy Spirit: 'But the natural man does not receive the things of the Spirit of God, for they are foolishness to him; nor can he know them, because they are spiritually discerned' (1 Cor. 2:14). Without the Holy Spirit, we cannot grasp who Christ is and what he has done for sinners. The Spirit knows the things of God (1 Cor. 2:11) and without him, we cannot be Christians (Rom. 8:9).

Both Paul and Jesus taught that the Spirit is a divine person whose essential work is to reveal Christ to his people. If a person be in Christ, he has the Spirit of God indwelling him. Jesus called the Spirit 'another Helper' or 'another Advocate' (John 14:16) — he is all that Jesus is. To have the Spirit in you (John 14:17) is equivalent to having the Father and the Son in you (John 14:23). Paul's teaching is very similar in Romans 8, where he says that the Spirit of God is the Spirit of Christ, and if anyone does not have the Spirit, he does not belong to Christ (Rom. 8:9).

The Holy Spirit helps the Christian to pray (Rom. 8:26-27; Eph. 2:18; 6:18), to worship (Phil. 3:3), to love and to fellowship (Rom. 5:5; Phil. 2:1), to use our God-given gifts for the good of others (1 Cor. 12) and to grow in holiness (Gal. 5:22-23). Like his Lord and Saviour, Paul was thoroughly trinitarian in his view of the Godhead. Hence he closed his second letter to the Corinthians with the familiar words: 'The grace of the Lord Jesus Christ, and the love of God, and the communion [or fellowship] of the Holy Spirit be with you all' (2 Cor. 13:14).

## The way of salvation

Paul makes it clear that it is God the Holy Spirit who works in the soul of the sinner and brings him or her to Christ in penitence and faith, to find salvation in him. It is God who first sets the sinner apart for himself, for by ourselves we would never seek God; our wills are by nature too hardened and stubborn to want to have anything to do with him (Rom. 3:11). But in his love, God has predestined a people for himself, a people whom he has loved from before the foundation of the world (Rom. 8:29-30; 9:6-24; Eph. 1:3-11; 1 Thess. 1:4; 2 Tim. 1:9). God brings his elect people to life (Col. 2:13; 2 Cor. 5:17), enables them to repent of sin (2 Tim. 2:25), grants them the gift of faith (Eph. 2:8; Phil. 1:29), acquits them of all their sin through faith in Christ (Rom. 3:21-24; 10:4; 2 Cor. 5:21; Phil. 3:9), adopts them into his family (Eph. 1:5; Rom. 8:15-17,29; Gal. 4:5-6), works to make them holier in this life (Rom. 8:29; Eph. 5:25-27; Titus 2:14), keeps them through every trial and tribulation (Rom. 8:33-34) and finally receives them into glory (Rom. 8:30-39).

There are those who declare that the scheme of salvation taught by Christ is a very different one from that proclaimed by the apostle Paul. Regarding the doctrine of predestination recorded in Romans 9, for example, David Cairns states, 'It is because Paul's verses indicate a view of God untrue to the revelation given by our Lord that we object to them. This god, then, is not the true God, or let us rather say that for the moment St Paul's understanding of God is imperfect.'[17] It seems, however, that it is Cairns' understanding that is less than satisfactory. One could hardly imagine a more predestinarian prayer than that uttered by our Lord in Matthew 11:25-27: 'I thank you, Father, Lord of heaven and earth, because you have hidden these things from the wise and prudent and have revealed them to babes. Even so, Father, for so it seemed good in your sight. All things have been delivered to me by my Father, and no one knows the Son except the Father. Nor does anyone know the Father except the Son, and he to whom the Son wills to reveal him.'

Jesus spoke the language of election: 'For false christs and false prophets will arise and show great signs and wonders, so as to deceive, if possible, even the elect' (Matt. 24:24). The elect are not those who have chosen God — true though that is — but those whom God has chosen. Only those whom the Father has given to the Son will come to him in faith (John 6:37; see John 17:2,6,9,11), for no one can come to Christ unless the Father draws him (John 6:44,65). This teaching was as offensive to the natural man in the first century as it is today, so many who had followed Jesus up until this time left him (John 6:66).

Although Jesus and Paul did not express themselves in identical ways, they taught the same gospel. Christ warned in his parables that it was the Pharisee in the temple (Luke 18:9-14), the grumbling elder brother to the prodigal son (Luke 15:28), and the hard worker in the vineyard (Matt. 20:1-16) who pursued a law of righteousness without attaining it, because they sought it by works rather than humbly receiving it by faith (Rom. 9:31-32). Christ came to call, not the righteous, but sinners (Mark 2:17). He was vilified by the Pharisees as 'a friend of tax collectors and sinners' (Matt. 11:19). He reached out to the lost and the ungodly in a way that offended those who considered themselves respectable and righteous before God and man (Luke 7:36-50; 15:1-32). Jesus even used the term 'justified', found so often in Paul's writings, to describe the acceptance of the penitent sinner by God (Luke 18:14). Faith in Christ brings salvation (Luke 7:50) and healing (Luke 8:48; 17:19; 18:42). Religious observance is unable to save anyone, for, as Christ told the Pharisees and Sadducees of his day, 'Assuredly, I say to you that tax collectors and harlots enter the kingdom of God before you. For John came to you in the way of righteousness, and you did not believe him; but tax collectors and harlots believed him; and when you saw it, you did not afterward relent and believe him' (Matt. 21:31-32). Different modes of expression do not mean different modes of thought; Jesus and Paul both proclaim, 'By God's free grace a sinner is saved through faith in Jesus Christ.'

God gives the sinner new life (John 3:3; 5:24) and adopts him into his family, so that he can call upon God as his Father in heaven (Matt. 6:9). The believer does not call God 'Father' in the same way that Christ does, but Christ could still tell his disciples, 'I am ascending to my Father and your Father, and to my God and your God' (John 20:17). As a corollary to this, Christ calls his followers his 'brethren' (Matt. 28:10; John 20:17). Earlier in his ministry, Jesus had stretched out his hand towards his disciples and declared, 'Here are my mother and my brothers! For whoever does the will of my Father in heaven is my brother and sister and mother' (Matt. 12:49-50).

Growth in holiness comes through being a branch attached to the true vine, which is Christ (John 15:1-6). The fruits of answered prayer, obedience, love and joy are found, not through self-help programmes, but through being spiritually nourished by Christ (John 15:7-17). Like Paul, Jesus teaches that the true Christian cannot fall away, although he may lose close fellowship with God. Nevertheless, the believer has Christ's promise: 'And I give them eternal life, and they shall never perish; neither shall anyone snatch them out of my hand' (John 10:28). The ones who in the judgement are shown not to belong to Christ are not those who knew him once but who then fell away. Rather, they are the ones to whom the Lord will say, 'I *never* knew you' (Matt. 7:22). On the other hand, those who are predestined will be glorified; they are loved from everlasting to everlasting.

# 7.
# Aspects of the Christian life in Jesus and Paul

One needs to remember that Paul's letters were usually written for specific occasions. The two Corinthian letters, for instance, were written because Paul faced so many problems with the unruly church at Corinth. This means that only rarely — for example, in Romans, where he wrote to a church he had not yet visited — does Paul systematically deal with the basic themes of Christian belief and practice. However, what he does say about the Christian life reveals his deep affinity with the teachings of Christ himself.

## The church

Many people in the West today are precariously armed with a watered-down version of Christianity — which C. S. Lewis said 'can only supply an ineffectual echo to the massive chorus of agreed and admitted unbelief'.[1] As a result, they believe what they want to believe and think it is Christian, rather than submitting to the clear teachings of Scripture. One area concerns the church. Some believe in the church as a substitute for believing in Christ; others seem to think that the church is some kind of post-Christian afterthought. Alfred Loisy, a Roman Catholic modernist from the early part of the twentieth century, once commented that 'Jesus announced the kingdom, and it was the Church that came.'[2] Loisy may not have meant it quite as negatively as it sounded, but it has become a common opinion.

The truth is that our Lord came not only to call individuals to himself, but to found a body of people which he called the church. Christ chose twelve apostles, very obviously to fulfil the roles that the twelve patriarchs did in Israel of old. There is thus a continuity between the people of God in the Old Testament and the people of God in the New Testament. The Lord Jesus told the apostle Peter, 'I will build my church, and the gates of Hades [or hell] shall not prevail against it' (Matt. 16:18). Steps for carrying out discipline have been given to each local church, and if a sinner proves recalcitrant, and refuses to listen to two or more Christian witnesses, the offence must be told to the church. 'But if he refuses even to hear the church, let him be to you like a heathen and a tax collector' (Matt. 18:17).

It is thus no betrayal of our Lord's purposes that the apostle Paul set up churches wherever he went. Nine of his thirteen epistles are written to churches rather than individuals. Like Jesus, Paul saw continuities (as well as some discontinuities) between Israel and the church. Gentile Christians have been grafted onto the Jewish olive tree (Rom. 11:16-24). God dwelt with his people Israel (Lev. 26:11-12), so too with the church (2 Cor. 6:16); those who are of Abraham belong to Christ (Gal. 3:7,29; see John 8:39); there is an Israel 'after the flesh' (1 Cor. 10:18), but the church is the true circumcision (Phil. 3:3); God had his chosen people in the Old Testament (Deut. 7:7-8), so too in the New Testament (Eph. 1:4); in short, the church is Israel, spiritually, not racially, understood (Rom. 2:28-29; Gal. 6:16).

This church is one in Christ (John 17:21), and Paul laboured hard that that unity would be expressed in its corporate life (e.g.1 Cor. 1-4; Eph. 2:14-18; 4:1-6; Phil. 1:27; 2:2).

## The church as a spiritual bride, body and temple

In the Old Testament God sometimes portrayed himself, whether explicitly or implicitly, as the Bridegroom, with the people of Israel as his bride (e.g. Ezek. 16:20; Hosea 1-3). Christ picked up this image and applied it to himself and his disciples: 'Can the friends of the bridegroom fast while the bridegroom is with them? As long as they have the bridegroom with them they cannot fast. But the days will come when the bridegroom will be taken away from them, and then they will fast in those days' (Mark 2:19-20). The same idea is found in the parable of the wise and foolish virgins who were waiting for the bridegroom to come (Matt. 25:1-13).

Paul too portrayed the church in these terms. He wrote to the Corinthians: 'For I am jealous for you with godly jealousy. For I have betrothed you to one husband, that I may present you as a chaste virgin to Christ' (2 Cor.11:2). Later, as is well known, he wrote of the church's relationship with Christ as analogous to that between a wife and her husband. He could even refer to Genesis 2:24: 'For this reason a man shall leave his father and mother and be joined to his wife, and the two shall become one flesh', and then add, 'This is a great mystery, but I speak concerning Christ and the church' (Eph. 5:31-32).

Even Paul's use of the body as an image of the church's relationship with Christ may go back to our Lord himself. Paul wrote, 'For as we have many members in one body, but all the members do not have the same function, so we, being many, are one body in Christ, and individually members of one another' (Rom. 12:4-5; cf. 1 Cor. 12) This identity between Christ and his people, so close that they are described as his body, is found in Christ's parable of the sheep and the goats. Christ will declare that inasmuch as the sheep have fed, clothed, tended and visited the least of his brethren, they have done so to Christ himself (Matt. 25:31-46). This has often been misunderstood to mean that we are to minister to every man, woman and child because Christ is to be seen in each one. In nineteenth-century England, F. D. Maurice used to teach that 'The truth is that every man is in Christ; the condemnation of every man is, that he will not own the truth.'[3] While it is true that Christians are to show practical kindness to all, whether Christians or not (see Luke 10:25-37; Gal. 6:10), it is also true that in Matthew 25 Jesus is referring specifically to Christians. The 'least of his brethren' are so closely identified with Christ that what is done to them is done to him.

Paul's dramatic conversion on the road to Damascus would also have contributed to the development of this view of the church as

Christ's body. As Paul (Saul) fell to the ground, he heard a voice saying to him, 'Saul, Saul, why are you persecuting me?' (Acts 9:4). In reply to the question, 'Who are you, Lord?' Paul received the answer: 'I am Jesus, whom you are persecuting' (Acts 9:5). Paul's conversion experience and the parable of the sheep and the goats would together explain how the church came to be viewed as the body of Christ.

Using yet another image, Christ spoke of himself in terms borrowed from the Old Testament as 'the stone which the builders rejected' and which had 'become the chief cornerstone' (Matt. 21:42; see Ps. 118:22). While Paul does not elaborate on this image in the way that Peter does in 1 Peter 2:6-8, he still uses the idea of Christ as the 'rejected stone' — 'a stumbling stone and rock of offence' (Rom. 9:33, from Isa. 8:14; 28:16). And in Ephesians he writes of Christ as 'the chief cornerstone, in whom the whole building, being joined together, grows into a holy temple in the Lord' (Eph. 2:20-21; see also 2 Cor. 6:16, where the church is referred to as a temple). The church is to be viewed as a temple built around the Lord Jesus Christ as the rejected chief cornerstone.

Both Jesus and Paul taught the essential spiritual nature of the people of God. Christ offended the Jews by saying that, although they were physically descended from Abraham, they were in fact of their father the devil. Those who are truly Abraham's children would do his works — they would believe the truth as it is in Jesus (John 8:33-47). It is the converted sinner who becomes a son of Abraham (Luke 19:9). Paul makes the same point when he says, 'And if you are Christ's, then you are Abraham's seed, and heirs according to the promise' (Gal. 3:29). A Christian is not one whose father was an elder and whose third cousin is a missionary; a Christian is one who, like Abraham, has been led to place his faith in Christ alone for salvation.

### Baptism and the Lord's Supper

It is clear that Paul did not invent the two Christian ordinances of baptism and the Lord's Supper. In his Epistle to the Romans, Paul asks, 'Or do you not know that as many of us as were baptized into Christ Jesus were baptized into his death?' (Rom. 6:3). He is not explaining baptism so much as assuming that the Roman Christians already understand it; he is simply reminding them of its meaning. There are many other Pauline references to baptism (1 Cor. 1:13-17; 10:1-13; Gal. 3:27; Eph. 5:26; Col. 2:12). Those who like to think that they are critical scholars often reject the historicity of Christ's command to baptize, given in Matthew 28:19-20. But Paul and the early Christian leaders all knew about baptism, undoubtedly from Christ's own lips (see Acts 2:38; 8:12,38; 10:47-48).

It is perhaps not surprising that Christ himself forges the link between baptism and his death on the cross. He declared, 'I have a baptism to be baptized with, and how distressed I am till it is accomplished!' (Luke 12:50; see Matt. 20:20-28). This would appear to be the most obvious explanation for the way Paul writes in Romans 6:3 — the apostle was referring to a teaching that was already familiar to his readers.

Something similar can be said of the Lord's Supper. All three Synoptic Gospels record its institution (Matt. 26:26-30; Mark 14:22-26; Luke 22:14-23) and Paul reports to the Corinthian church how it ought to be proclaiming the Lord's death till he comes (1 Cor. 11:23-26). Paul's teaching on the Lord's Supper is derived from the teaching and practice of the Lord himself.

## The call to the Gentiles

Paul is known as the apostle to the Gentiles, although the book of Acts tells us that he was not the initiator of the Gentile mission (see Acts 10-11). But the God who had separated Paul from his mother's womb ordained that he would preach Christ among the Gentiles (Gal. 1:15-16). As a result, he told the church at Rome: 'For I speak to you Gentiles; inasmuch as I am an apostle to the Gentiles, I magnify my ministry' (Rom. 11:13). He saw his mission as being to 'preach among the Gentiles the unsearchable riches of Christ' (Eph. 3:8) — a mission that was recognized by the other apostles, James, Peter and John (Gal. 2:7-9).

Yet Paul's missionary policy was always to preach to the Jew first, then the Greek (Rom. 1:16; cf. Acts 13:45-46; 18:5-6). His custom was to proclaim Jesus as the Christ to the synagogue before he turned to the Gentiles (Acts 13:5,14; 14:1; 16:13; 17:2-3; 19:8). It is perhaps surprising, but only two of Paul's speeches recorded in Acts are directed at specifically Gentile hearers — the rustic community at Lystra (Acts 14:8-20) and the sophisticated philosophers at Athens (Acts 17:16-34). Paul was an apostle to the Jews as well as to the Gentiles.

This fits in with the mission of our Lord himself. As Paul well knew, Christ was 'a servant to the circumcision for the truth of God, to confirm the promises made to the fathers' (Rom. 15:8). Because of this, Christ tended to confine his mission to working among the Jews. At the beginning of a preaching and healing tour, he told the twelve: 'Do not go into the way of the Gentiles, and do not enter a city of the Samaritans. But go rather to the lost sheep of the house of Israel' (Matt. 10:5-6). Commenting on these verses in Matthew 10, Charles H. H. Scobie considers that 'The conclusion is inescapable that the saying forbidding a mission to Samaritans or Gentiles was employed by a conservative Jewish-Christian community which stood in opposition to the outreach pioneered by the Hellenists.'[4] In fact, the conclusion is quite escapable. Jesus never intended these words to forbid for ever a mission to the Samaritans and Gentiles, and there is no way anyone armed with the Gospel of Matthew could have interpreted them — or misinterpreted them — in such a way. As is well known, Matthew concludes his Gospel with the ringing words of Jesus' Great Commission: 'Go therefore and make disciples of all the nations, baptizing them in the name of the Father and of the Son and of the Holy Spirit, teaching them to observe all things that I have commanded you; and lo, I am with you always, even to the end of the age' (Matt. 28:19-20).

Throughout Jesus' earthly ministry there were strong indications that the message of judgement and salvation would go out into the Gentile world. The Lord praised the faith of a Roman centurion, declaring that he had not seen its like in Israel (Matt. 8:10); demon-possessed men in places removed from the usual areas of Jewish settlement were healed (Matt. 8:28-34; Mark 5:1-20); the faith of a Syro-Phoenician woman is first tested, then praised (Matt. 15:21-28; Mark 7:24-30); it was declared that in his name Gentiles would put their trust (Matt. 12:21) for the gospel would be preached to all the nations (Matt. 24:14); and when a woman anointed Christ with expensive oil, he told those who objected, 'Assuredly, I say to you, wherever this gospel is preached in the whole world, what this woman has done will also be told as a memorial to her' (Matt. 26:13; Mark 14:9). Because of the refusal of the Jews to recognize Jesus as their Messiah, the kingdom of God would be taken from them and given to others (Matt. 21:43; Mark 12:1-12).

Luke records that when Christ preached at the synagogue in Nazareth, saying that the words of Isaiah 61:1-2 were fulfilled in him, the people marvelled at the gracious words which came from his lips. But when he went on to imply that God would call the Gentiles and save his elect from among them, just as he had in the days of Elijah (with the widow of Zarephath) and Elisha (with Namaan the Syrian), his hearers suddenly became filled with rage (Luke 4:16-30). The parable of the Good Samaritan teaches, among other things, that Samaritans were not beyond the pale of God's work of grace (Luke 10:25-37) — a lesson which is also to be found in the account of the healing of the ten lepers where only the Samaritan returned to give glory to God. Gentiles from the south and from Nineveh would rise up in the judgement and show that they had responded to far less light than had been granted to Israel (Luke 11:29-32).

The impetus behind the Gentile mission is to be found in the teaching and healing ministry of Christ himself. It was he who told the Jews: 'There will be weeping and gnashing of teeth, when you see Abraham and Isaac and Jacob and all the prophets in the kingdom of God, and yourselves thrust out. They will come from the east and the west, from the north and the south, and sit down in the kingdom of God' (Luke 13:28-29; Matt.8:11-12). Repentance and remission of sins in the name of Christ would therefore be preached to all nations, beginning at Jerusalem (Luke 24:47).

John's Gospel, too, is instructive on this issue. While salvation is of the Jews (John 4:22), it is not confined to them, and with the coming of Jesus as the Messiah, the temple at Jerusalem lost its centrality in God's scheme of things (John 4:21-24). The Greeks were not outside of Christ's saving interests (John 7:35; 12:20). Jesus specifically declared, 'And other sheep I have which are not of this fold; them also I must bring, and they will hear my voice; and there will be one flock and one shepherd' (John 10:16). The full implications of this are worked out by the apostle Paul in Ephesians 2:13-18, where he declares that the middle wall of division between Jew and Gentile has been broken down in Christ. The result is not a Jewish and a Gentile church, but one body of Christ.

Whereas the mission to the Gentiles did cause some consternation in the early church (see e.g. Acts 10; Gal. 2:11-14), Paul seems to have penetrated the mind of Christ more readily and deeply than most. Even the smallest of nuances are picked up by Paul. Christ prophesied, for example, that 'Jerusalem will be trampled by Gentiles until the times of the Gentiles are fulfilled' (Luke 21:24). The word 'until' (actually two words in the Greek) hints that more favourable times for the Jews may come when, as Paul puts it, 'the fulness of the Gentiles has come in' (Rom. 11:25). That, at any rate, may have been behind Paul's claim that the fall of the Jews is not the end of the story. God will extend his saving arm to Israel yet again (Rom. 11:11-26).

One must conclude that in the calling of the Gentiles, Paul and Jesus were one.


## Discipline in the church

As we have already seen, Christ established principles for carrying out discipline in the local church. The offender was first to be confronted privately about his sin, then with witnesses and, finally, if he proved intransigent, the church was to be told and to treat him as an outsider (Matt. 18:15-18). It cannot be said that those steps are obviously followed in the case of the incestuous man at Corinth (1 Cor. 5). The sin was public enough, so Paul seems to have leapt to the final step and called on the church to put the man outside of the fellowship. If 2 Corinthians 2:3-11 is referring to the same episode — something many scholars are strangely reluctant to concede — Paul says that the punishment was inflicted by 'the majority' (v.6, as in Matt. 18:17), and the man repented.

Discipline, however, was not to be taken too far. God alone would judge outsiders; that was not the church's task (1 Cor. 5:12-13). Paul also warned about being quick to judge another: 'Therefore judge nothing before the time, until the Lord comes, who will both bring to light the hidden things of darkness and reveal the counsels of the hearts; and then each one's praise will come from God' (1 Cor. 4:5). Even preachers with impure motives were not dealt with, provided they taught the truths of the gospel (Phil. 1:15-18).

All this is in keeping with the teaching of Christ, who warned us not to judge, lest we too be judged — i.e. we are not to judge in a carping, censorious way (Matt. 7:1). Self-righteous condemnations of the sins of others is a failing common to all of us, and Paul warns against it as vigorously as does Christ (Rom. 2:1). Both Paul and Jesus emphasized the need to humbly examine oneself first before presuming to point out the sins of others (Matt. 7:2-5; Gal. 6:1) and the need to heal broken relationships within the fellowship quickly (Matt. 5:23-24; Eph. 4:26). Obvious weeds are to be removed, but not so obvious tares are to be left in the field with the wheat (Matt. 13:24-30,36-43). To try to carry out the judgment too early will only do harm (Matt. 13:29). Those outside the church who openly reject the Son of Man are to be left to the judgement; we are not to call down fire from heaven upon them (Luke 9:51-56). While ultimately those who are not with Christ are against him (Matt. 12:30), it can nevertheless be true that 'He who is not against us is on our side' (Mark 9:40).

## Spiritual warfare

Many people today, whether biblical scholars or not, laugh at the notion that there may exist a created personal being who fell from grace and is bitterly opposed to God, and who leads an entourage of fallen angels known as demons. But both Paul and Jesus believed in their existence, and viewed them as the insidious enemies of the people of God. Just after his baptism, Christ was tempted three times by Satan (Matt. 4:1-11). When he taught his disciples to pray, 'But deliver us from evil', it is quite likely that the ambiguous expression meant: 'Deliver us from the Evil One' (Matt. 6:13). While Jesus healed many who were simply ill or incapacitated in some way, it is also true that he cast out demons. He did so without any indication that he was accommodating himself to the level of the ignorant multitude living before the advent of Newton and Darwin (e.g. Matt. 8:16,28-34; 9:32; 10:1; 12:22-30,43-45; 15:21-28; 17:14-21). Jesus also warned that it is the devil who has wrought havoc in the Lord's good creation (Matt.13:38-39); and it is he who seeks to keep fallen and needy sinners from responding to the Word of God (Matt. 13:19). He, for example, entered Judas Iscariot (Luke 22:3) and put it into his heart to betray the Son of Man (John 13:2). In a different way, he asked for Peter that he might sift him as wheat, but Christ's prayers would ultimately see Peter restored to fellowship with his Lord and useful service among his brethren (Luke 22:31-32).

Paul's message is no different. Satan is 'the god of this age' who has blinded those who do not believe in Christ (2 Cor. 4:4) — a description of the devil which is very close to Christ's own reference to him as 'the ruler of this world' (John 12:31; 14:30; 16:11). Paul knew that Satan was ever ready to take advantage of Christians, but he added: 'We are not ignorant of his devices' (2 Cor. 2:11). The serpent is a crafty and deceptive foe (2 Cor. 11:3) who works in the sons of disobedience (Eph. 2:2). Indeed, he is also the foe of Christians, who therefore need to put on the whole armour of God if they are to stand against his schemes (Eph. 6:10-18). The 'snare of the devil' is an ever-present threat, whether to opponents of the gospel (2 Tim. 2:26) or to potential elders in the church of Jesus Christ (1 Tim. 3:7).

Because of the reality of Satan and our own propensity to sin, the Christian is constantly engaged in spiritual warfare. This warfare is not a matter of swords and shields, for as Jesus informed Pilate, 'My kingdom is not of this world. If my kingdom were of this world, my servants would fight, so that I should not be delivered to the Jews; but now my kingdom is not from here' (John 18:36). Paul makes a similar point in his Corinthian correspondence: 'For though we walk in the flesh, we do not war according to the flesh. For the weapons of our warfare are not carnal but mighty in God for pulling down strongholds, casting down arguments and every high thing that exalts itself against the knowledge of God, bringing every thought into captivity to the obedience of Christ' (2 Cor. 10:3-5).

Alas, we are not always triumphant in this warfare. 'The flesh lusts against the Spirit, and the Spirit against the flesh; and these are contrary to one another, so that you do not do the things that you wish' (Gal. 5:17). Hence Paul found himself, even as a mature Christian believer and an apostle of Christ, failing to do the good that he wished to do and practising the evil that he wished not to (Rom. 7:13-25). At seventy-eight years of age, after a lifetime of what could only be described as devoted service in the cause of Christ, Andrew Bonar looked back over his life and wrote, 'Imperfection stamped on everything I ever undertook; omission running through my life.'[5] For the Christian, it is, as Jesus said, a matter of the spirit being willing, but the flesh being weak (Matt. 26:41).

## Love and law

Drawing from the Old Testament, Christ declared that the two great commandments were: 'You shall love the Lord your God with all your heart, with all your soul, and with all your mind,' and 'You shall love your neighbour as yourself' (Matt. 22:34-40; citing Deut. 6:5 and Lev. 19:18). On these two commandments hang all the Law and the Prophets (Matt. 22:40). At the same time Christ makes it clear that love does not abolish the law of God: 'Do not think that I came to destroy the Law or the Prophets. I did not come to destroy but to fulfil. For assuredly, I say to you, till heaven and earth pass away, one jot or one tittle will by no means pass from the law till all is fulfilled. Whoever therefore breaks one of the least of these commandments, and teaches men so, shall be called least in the kingdom of heaven; but whoever does and teaches them, he shall be called great in the kingdom of heaven' (Matt. 5:17-19). In telling the parable of the Good Samaritan and in speaking to the rich young ruler, the Lord pressed the need to obey God's law (Luke 10:28; Matt. 19:17). Love and law, rightly understood, are not contrary to one another. In fact, to quote Christ himself, 'If you love me, keep my commandments' (John 14:15; see also vv. 21,23).

Paul too emphasized the place of love, for 'Love is the fulfilment of the law' (Rom. 13:10; see Gal. 5:14). God himself teaches Christians to love one another in a brotherly way; this is basic to the community life of Christians (1 Thess. 4:9). We are to 'bear one another's burdens, and so fulfil the law of Christ' (Gal. 6:2). Here Paul may be referring to the general thrust of Christ's teaching, or he may have a specific text in mind, perhaps that which was incorporated into John 13:34: 'A new commandment I give to you, that you love one another; as I have loved you, that you also love one another.'

With regard to the law, the Christian has been delivered from it (Rom. 7:6), for Christ is the end of the law, meaning he is its fulfilment and goal more than its termination (Rom. 10:4). The law as a means of salvation is wiped out by the cross (Col. 2:14) and the ceremonial commandments that separated Jew from Gentile are abolished (Eph. 2:15). But love and law are compatible — keeping the commandments of God (1 Cor. 7:19) is akin to faith working through love (Gal. 5:6). Although justification is by faith alone in Christ alone, this does not mean that the law is made void; on the contrary, it is established (Rom. 3:31). In itself, the law is designed to bring life (Rom. 7:10); it is holy, just and good (Rom. 7:12); it is spiritual (Rom. 7:14). The law shows us our need of Christ, and having trusted in him, shows us how to live for him. 'For what the law could not do in that it was weak through the flesh, God did by sending his own Son in the likeness of sinful flesh, on account of sin: he condemned sin in the flesh, that the righteous requirement of the law might be fulfilled in us who do not walk according to the flesh but according to the Spirit' (Rom. 8:3-4).

### Grace leads to graciousness

In the parable of the unforgiving servant, Christ makes the point that those who claim to have received the grace of God in Christ ought in turn to be gracious and forgiving towards those who have wronged them in much smaller ways (Matt. 18:21-35). The Christian needs to be much aware of his debt to grace. To cite the godly Robert Murray M'Cheyne:

> Even on earth, as through a glass,
> Darkly, let thy glory pass;
> Make forgiveness feel so sweet;
> Make thy Spirit's help so meet;
> Even on earth, Lord, make me know
> Something of how much I owe.[6]

The one who realizes he has been forgiven much will exhibit this by loving much (Luke 7:36-50). Paul's message is the same but the language is more compressed: 'And be kind to one another, tender-hearted, forgiving one another, just as God in Christ also forgave you' (Eph. 4:32).

Such an overflow of grace will entail less demanding of our rights and more concern to minister to others. Such an outlook will even be seen in our evangelistic approach. In the middle of a long section on how he did not make use of rights that he in fact possessed (1 Cor. 8-10), Paul remarks, 'For though I am free from all men, I have made myself a servant to all, that I might win the more; and to the Jews I became as a Jew, that I might win Jews; to those who are under the law, as under the law, that I might win those who are under the law; to those who are without law, as without law (not being without law toward God, but under law toward Christ), that I might win those who are without law; to the weak I became as weak, that I might win the weak. I have become all things to all men, that I might by all means save some.' Then he explains: 'Now this I do for the gospel's sake, that I may be partaker of it with you' (1 Cor. 9:19-23).

Teaching that is biblical ought not to be defined as dishing up an interminable series of sermons on the intricacies of Daniel 11. Paul preached the same gospel to the Jews (Acts 13) as he did to the Gentiles (Acts 17), but he did it in a way that was appropriate to each group. We find the same consideration in Christ. Our Lord spoke in parables, partly to keep his word from those who were not elect (Mark 4:10-12), but when he spoke to his disciples, he did so only 'as they were able to hear it' (Mark 4:33). Later, he told them, 'I still have many things to say to you, but you cannot bear them now' (John 16:12). That is part of what it means to 'speak the truth in love' (Eph. 4:15).

Having died to sin and self (Mark 8:34; John 12:24-25; 2 Cor. 5:14-15; Gal. 5:24), the Christian is freed to serve Christ first of all (Luke 14:26; Phil. 3:8). The Christian's primary aim is therefore not to please men (Matt. 22:16; Gal. 1:10), but, having placed the claims of Christ first, the Christian will seek to 'please all men in all things ... that they may be saved' (1 Cor.10:33).

## Indignation at sin, compassion for the sinner

Those who trust in their own righteousness must necessarily despise others (Luke 18:9). The Christian gospel is not a legal ladder into heaven. As we saw in the previous chapter, it was Christ himself who criticized the Pharisees on this very issue: 'Assuredly, I say to you that tax collectors and harlots enter the kingdom of God before you. For John came to you in the way of righteousness, and you did not believe him; but tax collectors and harlots believed him; and when you saw it, you did not afterward relent and believe him' (Matt. 21:31-32). Using more theological terminology, Paul says the same thing: 'What shall we say then? That Gentiles, who did not pursue righteousness, have attained to righteousness, even the righteousness of faith; but Israel, pursuing the law of righteousness, has not attained to the law of righteousness. Why? Because they did not seek it by faith, but as it were, by the works of the law' (Rom. 9:30-32). The tragic error of the Jews is that 'They being ignorant of God's righteousness, and seeking to establish their own righteousness, have not submitted to the righteousness of God' (Rom. 10:3). As the great Blaise Pascal put it, 'There are only two kinds of men: the righteous who think they are sinners and the sinners who think they are righteous.'[7]

God's righteousness is seen in his law and in his grace; and seen most perfectly at Calvary where his love and justice met — his righteous law was fulfilled that free grace might be extended to sinners. Hence God can be both just and the justifier of the one who has faith in Jesus (Rom. 3:25-26). This has implications for the character of the Christian. Because of God's righteous laws, the Christian hates sin; but because of God's righteous grace, the Christian is compassionate to the sinner. Something of this can be seen, in different ways, in the lives of Jesus and Paul.

Christ Jesus knew what it was to burn with indignation at sin. Twice, at the beginning and at the end of his public ministry, he cleared the money-changers out of the temple (John 2:13-17; Mark 11:15-19). The hardness of heart of those in the synagogue aroused the twin responses of grief and anger in his heart (Mark 3:5). Christ never regarded sin lightly, and his warnings on the subject could be severe indeed: 'But whoever causes one of these little ones who believe in me to sin, it would be better for him if a millstone were hung around his neck, and he were drowned in the depth of the sea' (Matt.18:6).

Yet Christ also wept when he thought of how Jerusalem had rejected the gospel of peace and of how this would lead to her destruction, which took place in A.D. 70 when the Roman armies devastated the city (Luke 19:41-44). Matthew and Mark tell us that 'When he saw the multitudes, he was moved with compassion for them, because they were weary and scattered, like sheep having no shepherd' (Matt. 9:36; Mark 6:34). The sight of the multitudes, many of them sick, moved him with compassion for them (Matt. 14:14). Described in prophecy as 'a man of sorrows and acquainted with grief' (Isa. 53:3), Christ groaned in the spirit and was troubled before the tomb of his friend Lazarus (John 11:33). The Greek word used there is found in extra-biblical Greek to describe the snorting of horses. Jesus seems to have been almost outraged at the havoc that sin has caused in the world. This anger was combined with grief, so two verses later we come to the clipped but powerful statement that 'Jesus wept.'

Paul too could combine indignation at sin with compassion for sinners. He asked, 'Who is made to stumble, and I do not burn with indignation?' (2 Cor. 11:29). In an outburst that has attracted squeals of outrage from the selective moralism of biblical critics, Paul wrote to the Galatian churches: 'As for those agitators, I wish they would go the whole way and emasculate themselves!' (Gal. 5:12, NIV). The Galatian churches had been troubled by legalistic teachers who were saying that the work of Christ was not enough for salvation; one had to add circumcision to the cross. Paul's response is obviously sarcastic, and a result of his deep love for the truths of grace. It is not immediately obvious that its spirit is far removed from Christ's words, cited earlier, in Matthew 18:6. And it seems almost mild when compared with the holy violence of Christ's denunciation of the scribes and Pharisees in Matthew 23.

But if Paul's soul was provoked by the depths of human sin (see Acts 17:16), it was also moved with compassion at the predicament of sinners. When he wrote of those whom he referred to as 'the enemies of the cross of Christ', he could not do so without weeping (Phil. 3:18). He thought of what it would mean for a human being, alone and stained with sin, to face God, who is a consuming fire, without having taken refuge in the cross of Christ. John Newton could face that prospect:

> O wondrous love! to bleed and die,
> To bear the cross and shame,
> That guilty sinners such as I,
> Might plead thy gracious name![8]

But millions reject the 'gracious name'. It is small wonder that concern at the spiritual state of his fellow human beings caused Paul much affliction and anguish of heart, together with many tears (2 Cor. 2:4; Acts 20:19,31).

This peculiar combination of indignation and compassion, strength and meekness, power and tenderness, is born of an outlook which takes seriously what it means to be a human being, created in the image of God and accountable to him. The combination is rare, but it has never been better described than in the words of F. J. Chavasse, used to pay tribute to J. C. Ryle, his predecessor as the Bishop of Liverpool. Chavasse portrayed Ryle as 'that man of granite with the heart of a child'.[9]

There is, of course, one vital difference between Jesus and Paul on this matter. Paul felt his indignation burn at his own sin. He knew the frustrations of seeking perfection while falling short of it: 'O wretched man that I am! Who will deliver me from this body of death?' (Rom. 7:24). Paul knew himself to be the least of the apostles (1 Cor. 15:9), less than the least of all the saints (Eph. 3:8), and, in fact, the chief of sinners (1 Tim. 1:15). Christ knew no sin, for the ruler of this world had nothing in him (John 14:30).

## The use of worldly wealth

Warnings about the sin of covetousness abound in Scripture. One of the most striking examples is Jesus' parable of the rich fool. This fool accumulates all the wealth he can, and then sits back in the hope of enjoying the easy life. 'But God said to him, "You fool! This night your soul will be required of you; then whose will those things be which you have provided?" So is he who lays up treasure for himself, and is not rich toward God' (Luke 12:20-21). The lesson was not lost on the apostle Paul who pointed out to young Timothy: 'For we brought nothing into this world, and it is certain we can carry nothing out' (1 Tim. 6:7). He went on: 'Command those who are rich in this present age not to be haughty, nor to trust in uncertain riches but in the living God, who gives us richly all things to enjoy. Let them do good, that they be rich in good works, ready to give, willing to share, storing up for themselves a good foundation for the time to come, that they may lay hold on eternal life' (1 Tim. 6:17-19).

As a result, generous giving is to be a feature of the Christian's

life. Christ exhorted, 'Give, and it will be given to you' (Luke 6:38).
The widow who gave sacrificially is commended more than those
who gave out of their abundance (Mark 12:41-44). Paul also
commends giving that is born of faith (2 Cor. 8:5), and is cheerfully
sacrificial and voluntary (2 Cor. 8:3; 9:7).

### Living in a hostile world

In a general way, Jesus told his disciples that they would live in the
world without being of it (John 17:14-18). They were to operate as
salt, light and leaven in the world (Matt. 5:13; 13:33). As Paul
applied these principles to Christians in various parts of the Roman
Empire, he urged: 'Brethren, let each one remain with God in that
calling in which he was called' (1 Cor. 7:24). This could mean
working away quietly at one's own business (1 Thess. 4:11); it
certainly did not mean giving up work (2 Thess. 3:6-12). There is no
revolutionary call, for example, to rise up against the institution of
slavery (Philem. 12,14), nor is there any monastic retreat from
rubbing shoulders with unbelieving sinners in the day-to-day world
(1 Cor. 5:9-12).

Suffering and persecution are inevitable for the Christian (Matt.
5:10-12; John 15:18-20; 2 Tim. 3:12). But any suffering is but for
a short time, rather like what is endured by a woman in labour — joy
is not far away (John 16:21). As Paul put it, 'I consider that the
sufferings of this present time are not worthy to be compared with
the glory which shall be revealed in us' (Rom. 8:18; see 2 Cor.3:18).
Christians may suffer terribly, but they are joint-heirs with Christ
(Rom. 8:17; John 17:22-24). One moment in glory will more than
compensate for all the miseries faced on this earth.

### Judgement by works

Finally, we need to be clear that this life has eternal consequences.
Christ declared that he will come as the Son of Man in the glory of

his Father with his angels, and 'reward each according to his works' (Matt. 16:27). Those who have done good will rise to the resurrection of life, and those who have done evil to the resurrection of condemnation (John 5:29). This doctrine is taught in the Old Testament (e.g. Ps. 62:12; Prov. 24:12), and also by the apostle Paul (Rom. 2:5-10; 1 Cor. 3:10-15; 2 Cor. 5:10). Justification is by faith, not works; but judgement is according to works. The first work we need to do is given us by Christ: 'This is the work of God, that you believe in him whom he sent' (John 6:29).

# 8.
# Paul and the other apostles

It is customary today to portray various schools of thought — 'circles' is the usual term for them — as having been at work in the apostolic period. Often these are considered to have developed different theologies which managed to co-exist back in the first century. The implication is that we ought not to be threatened by the existence of Catholic, Reformed, Pentecostal and liberal versions of Christianity. Such an approach owes much to the work of Ferdinand Christian Baur, who was Professor of Theology at Tübingen in Germany for thirty-four years until his death in 1826. Following Hegel's conception of history, Baur portrayed Paul as being violently opposed to Peter, with the book of Acts producing a synthesis which glossed over these differences and harmonized them. Closer to our own times, Lloyd Gaston has stated that the theology of Paul and the theology of the Jerusalem church were 'completely different'.[1]

This theory has been taken far more seriously than it deserves. There were tensions in the early church, to be sure. Paul and Barnabas contended with one another over whether to take John Mark with them again on the second missionary journey (Acts 15:37-40); Paul's missionary work among the Gentiles caused some consternation for Jewish Christians who had to live with their kinsmen in Jerusalem (Acts 21:15-25); the Corinthian church seems to have been split into four factions (1 Cor. 1-4); and at Antioch Paul had to publicly rebuke Peter for betraying his gospel principles by withdrawing from table fellowship with the Gentiles (Gal. 2:11-14). All this is what one would expect in a sinful, fallen world.

What is clear is that Paul was known and accepted by the other apostles and early Christian leaders, and that he had plenty of opportunities to tap sources of information about Jesus the Christ. Paul trusted the other apostles to preach the same gospel as he did. That is why he did not make the journey to Rome — because the gospel had already reached there. Hence Paul wrote, 'And so I have made it my aim to preach the gospel, not where Christ was named, lest I should build on another man's foundation' (Rom.15:20). Even at Corinth, where the church was split into four parties, Paul was at pains to emphasize that there should be no divisions between true Christians. One group was claiming to belong to Paul, another to Apollos, another to Cephas (Peter), and another to Christ (1 Cor. 1:12). Some of the Corinthian converts may well have preferred the more eloquent preaching of Apollos, so Paul had to correct their thinking: 'Who then is Paul, and who is Apollos, but ministers through whom you believed, as the Lord gave to each one? I planted, Apollos watered, but God gave the increase. So then neither he who plants is anything, nor he who waters, but God who gives the increase' (1 Cor. 3:5-7). Paul's point is that there was division where there ought to have been humble co-operation and mutual recognition. But it is clearly false to paint a picture of Paul's being at doctrinal loggerheads with Peter or Apollos.

Referring to the other apostles, Paul could say, 'Therefore, whether it was I or they, so we preach and so you believed' (1 Cor. 15:11). The apostles were united in their adherence to Christ and his one gospel of grace. This can be seen even in the book of Galatians, where Paul affirms most vigorously his independent apostleship, which came 'not from men nor through man, but through Jesus Christ and God the Father who raised him from the dead' (Gal. 1:1). When Paul was called to be an apostle, he 'did not immediately confer with flesh and blood' (Gal. 1:16). He did not need the *imprimatur* of any other apostle or bishop of bishops. For quite a while, Paul's face was unknown to the churches of Judea (Gal. 1:22). It was only after three years that he went up to Jerusalem to see Peter (Cephas), and remained with him fifteen days (Gal. 1:18). Referring to this meeting, C. H. Dodd has remarked rather laconically that 'We may presume they did not spend all the time talking about the weather.'² Paul also met with James, the Lord's brother (Gal. 1:19). The 'last apostle' (1 Cor. 15:8) was certainly not in need of information about Christ — for he waited three years before he sought out Peter and James — but he was concerned to maintain the unity of the fellowship.

Fourteen years later Paul again went up to Jerusalem, and this time he met with Peter, James and John. They added nothing to Paul (Gal. 2:6). Unlike Apollos when he met with Priscilla and Aquila, Paul had no need to have the way of God explained to him more accurately (Acts 18:24-26). Yet, for all his independence, Paul still considered it important, even vital, that he possessed the approval of his fellow apostles. He wrote, 'And I went up by revelation, and communicated to them that gospel which I preach among the Gentiles, but privately to those who were of reputation, lest by any means I might run, or had run, in vain' (Gal. 2:2). As a result, he was more than happy when Peter, James and John extended the right hand of fellowship to Barnabas and himself (Gal. 2:9). Paul had abundant opportunity to acquaint himself with those apostles who had heard, seen and touched the Lord during the incarnation.

The apostles did not work in isolation from one another; there was a network of connections between them, and they met at least once in formal council (Acts 15). Silas (or Silvanus), for instance, is said to have helped Paul and Timothy to write the two epistles to the Thessalonians (1 Thess. 1:1; 2 Thess. 1:1), although it is clear that Paul was the main author (see 1 Thess. 2:18; 3:1-2; 4:13; 5:1,27; 2 Thess. 3:17). Peter also mentions him: 'By Silvanus, our faithful brother as I consider him, I have written to you briefly, exhorting and testifying that this is the true grace of God in which you stand' (1 Peter 5:12). Silas thus worked in close co-operation with both Peter and Paul.

There is a similar link in the person of John Mark. Paul's early experience with Mark was less than happy, with Mark leaving Paul and Barnabas at Perga in Pamphylia, perhaps being overcome by homesickness or perhaps disliking the idea of Gentiles being brought into the kingdom (Acts 13:13). Paul's later experience was much happier, and Mark is referred to with warm appreciation in Colossians 4:10 and Philemon 24. In 2 Timothy 4:11 Mark is said by Paul to be 'useful to me for ministry'. The apostle Peter writes in even more affectionate terms of 'Mark my son' (1 Peter 5:13). It is recorded by Eusebius of Cæsarea that the early Christian writer known as Papias considered that Mark was Peter's interpreter. Mark, in his Gospel, 'wrote down carefully, but not in order, all that he remembered of the Lord's sayings and doings'.[3]

The place of Luke is equally instructive. Luke occasionally travelled with the apostle (hence the 'we' passages which begin in Acts 16:10; 20:5; 27:1), and is referred to by Paul as 'the beloved physician' in Colossians 4:14. He is also mentioned in Philemon 24, and is said to have stood by Paul in his last days before his execution (2 Tim. 4:11). Luke came to write the two-volume work Luke and Acts, which, perhaps surprisingly, makes up more of the New Testament than Paul's thirteen letters combined. But in fact Luke may have already written his Gospel. The book of Acts finishes its story about the year A.D. 62, before Paul was put to death under the emperor Nero. The only reasonable explanation for Luke's not mentioning Paul's execution was that it had not yet taken place when he composed Acts. If Acts was written about A.D. 62, the Gospel of Luke, as volume one of the whole work, must have been written earlier.

The conclusion reached is that Paul knew the author of one Gospel (John), was quite well acquainted with the authors of two Gospels (Mark, Luke), knew Peter and James, and worked closely with men who worked with the other apostles (Luke, Mark, Barnabas).[4] In all this, there is no indication that Paul's gospel was deficient in any way or that he was at odds on any matter of faith or practice with any of the other apostles. Much earlier, we noted that, although Peter conceded that Paul's writings could be hard to understand at times, they did rank with 'the rest of the Scriptures' (2 Peter 3:15-16).

It is worth our while now to look briefly at epistles written by

New Testament writers besides Paul. Here we find that James, Peter and John and the anonymous author of the epistle to the Hebrews wrote letters which, like those of Paul, have few direct quotations of the words of Jesus or reports of what he did during his earthly ministry. But they nevertheless make it clear that they knew the Gospel accounts. Such a resemblance to Paul makes it unreasonable to expect Paul to have been any different in his epistles.

## Hebrews

We will assume that Hebrews came from the pen of someone besides the apostle Paul. What is more certain is that the author knew a good deal about the life of Jesus Christ. He knew of his temptations (Heb. 2:18; 4:15; cf. Matt. 4:1-11); his sufferings (2:10); his anguish in the Garden of Gethsemane (5:7; Matt. 26:36-46); his life of learning obedience to God through suffering (5:8); his descent from the tribe of Judah (7:14; Matt. 1:3); and that he was put to death outside Jerusalem (13:12; Matt. 27:32). One could not write a biography of Christ from the information in Hebrews, but the author drew on details of Christ's life when his purposes required it.

## James

In one of his less temperate outbursts, Martin Luther once complained that the Epistle of James had little of the gospel in it. Yet it is studded with allusions to Christ's words, in a much more pervasive way than are Paul's writings. There is an obvious reference to Jesus' words on oaths (Matt. 5:33-37) in James 5:12: 'But above all, my brethren, do not swear, either by heaven or by earth or with any other oath. But let your "Yes" be "Yes", and your "No", "No", lest you fall into judgement [or, just possibly, hypocrisy].'

A host of other allusions can be pointed out. Counting it joy when you face trials (1:2) is close to Matthew 5:11-12.God's preparedness to respond to our asking (1:5) reflects Matthew 7:7-8. Asking in faith without doubting (1:6) seems to be based on Mark 11:23-24. God's giving of good gifts to his children (1:17) is taught by Jesus in Matthew 7:11. Being doers of the Word and not hearers only (1:22) is close to Matthew 7:24 and Luke 11:28. God's choosing of the poor (2:5) is found in Luke 6:20. The royal law of 'You shall love your neighbour as yourself' (2:8) harks back to Matthew 22:39 (as well as Leviticus 19:18). The fact that a tree bears appropriate fruit is a theme common to James 3:12 and Matthew 7:16. The exalting of the humble (4:10) is much emphasized by our Lord (Matt. 23:12; Luke 14:11; 18:14). Not judging others (4:11-12) goes back to Matthew 7:1. Omitting to do what one knows is right (4:17) reminds the reader of Luke 12:47. The woes coming to those with riches are found in James 5:1 and Luke 6:24. The destructive power of moths on garments is in James 5:2 and Matthew 6:19-20. And restoring a sinner (5:19) is in harmony with Christ's words in Matthew 18:15-17.

Other possible references might be raised. The fact that we are to 'receive with meekness the implanted word' (1:21) surely is a concept which goes back to the parable of the sower (Matt. 13:1-9). In James 1:12 we read that the Lord has promised the crown of life to those who love him. This promise is not found in so many words in the Old Testament, so James Adamson suggests that we have here an otherwise unrecorded saying of Jesus.[5] This suggestion receives some confirmation from the fact that the saying is found in 1 Corinthians 9:25; 1 Peter 5:4; 2 Timothy 4:8 and Revelation 2:10.

## 1 Peter

A look at 1 Peter reveals similar results. The Christian's experience of being born again (1:3) must be based on the teaching found in John 3:3,7. The imperishable future reward of 1:4 is reminiscent of Luke 12:33. Not seeing Jesus but being blessed (1:8) reminds us of John 20:29. The prophets of old proclaiming the sufferings and glory of the Christ (1:10-12) goes back to Luke 24:25-26. The command to love one another in 1:22 and 4:8 reflects Jesus' teaching in John 13:34-35; 15:12. The 'rejected stone' metaphor of 2:4-8 is an elaboration of what is found in Mark 12:10. The good works of Christians leading to non-Christians being moved to glorify God is common to 2:12 and Matthew 5:16. The Christian's freedom being compatible with honouring the civil authorities (1:13-17) raises the same issues that Christ raised in paying the temple tax (Matt.17:26-7). The rhetorical questions of 2:20 must go back to Luke 6:32-34. The shepherd/sheep picture (2:25; 5:4) recalls Christ's own use of the imagery in Matthew 26:31 and John 10:11,14. Being blessed for suffering for righteousness' sake (3:14) is clearly harking back to Matthew 5:10. And the Christian view of serving leadership (5:3-5) is based on Christ's teaching in Luke 22:25-30.

Peter's general message of rejoicing in suffering, committing oneself to God, enduring unjust treatment, loving one's brothers, being humble and watching and praying unto the end shows how saturated he was with the teachings of his Master.[6]

Peter's second epistle also refers back to Christ's life (e.g. the transfiguration in 2 Peter 1:16-18) and words (e.g. 'the thief in the night' image in 2 Peter 3:10). The apostles were not in the business of devising 'cunningly devised fables' for they were eyewitnesses of Christ's majesty (2 Peter 1:16). Stories and sayings were not made up about Christ just because they might prove to be an inspiration to those who heard them. Despite the wild claims of many biblical critics, the apostles and the whole early Christian community believed that edification must be firmly based on truth.

## 1 John

1 John is also well-grounded in Gospel soil. The beatific vision of 1 John 3:1-2 combines the notions of seeing God and being his children, which are found together in Matthew 5:8-9. Testing the spirits (4:1) is something enjoined on us by our Lord himself (Matt. 7:15-20; 24:11,24). The claim that God's commandments are not burdensome (5:3) is an echo of Christ's words in Matthew 11:30.

Also the wholehearted belief that God will hear and answer prayer (5:15) harks back to Jesus' teaching in Mark 11:24.

Not surprisingly, 1 John is closer to John's Gospel in its parallels. To have Christ is to have life, and not to have him is not to have life (5:12; see John 3:36). The call to love God and others and keep the commandments (2:3-5; 3:23; 4:20-21; 5:3) is found in John 14:15,21,23-24; 15:10-12. The reference to joy being full (1:4) is an echo of John 15:11. And the apostolic awareness of possessing the Spirit of truth (4:6) is based on Christ's words in John 14:26; 16:13. Furthermore, many words recur in both the Gospel and the epistle, notably, 'life', 'truth', 'love', 'joy', 'light', 'darkness', 'the world', 'commandment(s)', 'testimony', and 'know'.


**References to Jesus' person, life and work**

The most determined unbeliever searches in vain to drive a wedge between Paul and the other apostles in their views of Jesus' person, life and work. There are some problems with the text of James 2:1, but Jesus is probably referred to as 'the Lord of glory'. Peter applies Isaiah 8:14, which speaks of Jehovah, to Christ in 1 Peter 2:8, which could only be valid if Peter viewed Christ as fully divine. In 2 Peter 1:1 Jesus Christ is called 'our God and Saviour'. Hebrews is particularly clear about the deity of Christ: he is the Creator (1:3, 10-12); angels worship him (1:6); he is called God (1:8); he is sinless (4:15; 7:26); and he is eternal (1:10-12; 13:8). John too speaks of him as the Word of life which was from the beginning (1 John 1:1) and as the true God (5:19).

Both Peter and John point very specifically to the life of Jesus. Peter says that Christ left us an example in the way he suffered (1 Peter 2:21-23). He obviously expects his readers to be familiar with the account of Christ's passion. John writes most bluntly of that 'which we have heard, which we have seen with our eyes, which we have looked upon, and our hands have handled' (1 John 1:1). Some think John was referring to the gospel, but the description is so physical that it surely refers to our Lord himself. John goes on to write that

'He who says he abides in him ought himself also to walk just as he walked' (1 John 2:6). Again, it is clear that John expects his readers to be familiar with the life and example of Jesus.

Hebrews speaks of Christ's having shared in our flesh and blood in order to save flesh and blood (2:14). Our Lord's true humanity is a most necessary part of the scheme of salvation: 'Therefore, in all things he had to be made like his brethren, that he might be a merciful and faithful High Priest in things pertaining to God, to make propitiation for the sins of the people' (2:17). The unknown author had a picture in his mind of Christ in his humanity living upon this earth, and he expected his readers to already share that picture.

The death of Christ is emphasized as the basis of the gospel message of salvation. Peter says that Christ was an example to us, but also that he himself 'bore our sins in his own body on the tree, that we, having died to sins, might live for righteousness — by whose stripes you were healed' (1 Peter 2:24). The supreme example is also the substitute who suffered as 'the just for the unjust' (1 Peter 3:18). John says that Christ is the propitiation for our sins (1 John 2:2; 4:10), meaning that he took upon himself the holy anger of God against sinners. Only in this way could God's justice be satisfied. The book of Hebrews devotes chapters to explaining how Christ is the superior High Priest and his sacrifice is perfect and once for all, unlike the repeated sacrifices carried out by the Old Testament priests (Heb. 7-10). Like 1 John, Hebrews uses the word 'propitiation' to describe the meaning of Jesus' sacrifice (2:17). James' book has a different purpose; it is like a New Testament book of Proverbs which tells Christians how they are to live their lives. It deals more with gospel living, and hence does not expound the inner workings of the gospel itself. Even so, the basis is faith in Christ, but this needs to be exemplified in the doing of good works (James 2:22).

The point remains that the apostles were not islands of influence which had no connection with one another. There were many interconnections and opportunities to pass on information about the Lord, if needed. Behind the diversity of style and expression, there is a coherent unity of message. They saw themselves as being united. Jude, for example, writes to his readers, 'But you, beloved, remember the words which were spoken before by the apostles of our Lord Jesus Christ: how they told you that there would be mockers in the last time who would walk according to their own ungodly lusts' (Jude 17-18). Jude's readers had access to more books than simply the book of Jude (see Acts 20:29-30; 1 Tim. 4:1-3; 2 Tim. 3:1-6; 2 Peter 3:3). This is precisely what one finds in Paul also (Col. 4:16; 1 Thess. 5:27). The epistles were not designed to be the preserve of one community; they were written to be copied and passed on to other communities of Christians.

The purpose of an epistle was not to repeat what was already known from a Gospel or Gospel tradition; it was to interpret and apply that teaching. Hence there are enough references to the Gospel tradition to show that it was known, but only parts of that tradition immediately relevant to the author's occasion are referred to and explained.

# 9.
# Paul as Christ's ambassador

Paul presents himself as an ambassador of Christ with a message urging sinners to be reconciled to God through Christ (2 Cor. 5:20). As Günther Bornkamm explains, 'Through the mouth of the ambassador Christ or God himself speaks...The focus is on the authority of the message rather than that of the one who conveys it.'[1] Paul was no innovator or corrupter of the gospel message entrusted to him. He reveals that he knew at least an outline of Christ's life and character; he knew and cited some of Christ's own words; he alludes to many more; his basic gospel message is in harmony with that of his Master; his references to other aspects of the Christian life are also in agreement with the teachings of the Master; and his ministry was accepted by the other apostles.

In his teachings and in his very lifestyle of authoritative yet humble service, Paul followed Christ. In every respect, Paul was one who could say, 'For I received from the Lord that which I also delivered to you' (1 Cor. 11:23) and 'I delivered to you first of all that which I also received' (1 Cor. 15:3). Modern biblical scholars are in love with the idea of innovation and novelty. Paul had a higher love; his ardent desire was to be a faithful ambassador of the Lord Jesus Christ. In this he succeeded. To know Christ, we need to know the Christ whom Paul reveals.

# References

**Chapter 1 — Jesus and Paul: an introduction**
1. Henri Troyat, *Tolstoy,* Penguin, Harmondsworth, 1970, p.815.
2. W. Wrede, *Paul,* Philip Green, London, 1907, p.179.
3. *Ibid.,* p.180.
4. Cited in H. Rollmann, *'Paulus alienus:* William Wrede on Comparing Jesus and Paul' in P. Richardson and J. C. Hurd (eds), *From Jesus to Paul: Studies in Honour of Francis Wright Beare,* Wilfrid Laurier University Press, Ontario, 1984, p.41.
5. R. Morgan, *The Nature of New Testament Theology,* SCM, London, 1973, p.60.
6. J. D. G. Dunn, *Unity and Diversity in the New Testament,* SCM, London, 1977, p.75.
7. John Wenham, *Easter Enigma,* Paternoster, Exeter, 1984, pp.112-16.
8. W. G. Kümmel, *Introduction to the New Testament,* SCM, London, 1975, pp. 120,98,151.
9. J. Wenham, *Redating Matthew, Mark and Luke: A Fresh Assault on the Synoptic Problem,* Hodder and Stoughton, London, 1991, note pp.xxii, 243.
10. J. A. T. Robinson, *Redating the New Testament,* SCM, London, 1976, p.282.
11. F. F. Bruce, 'Paul and the Historical Jesus' in *Bulletin of the John Rylands University Library,* vol. 56, 1974, p.335.
12. See D. Guthrie, *New History Introduction,* IVP, Illinois, 1990; D. A. Carson, D. J. Moo, and L. Morris, *An Introduction to the New Testament,* Zondervan, Michigan, 1992.
13. C. S. Lewis, *Fern-Seed and Elephants and other Essays on Christianity,* Fontana, Glasgow, 1975, p.106.

14. *Ibid.,* p.117.

15. *Ibid.,* p.125. Another worthwhile book on this subject is Eta Linnemann, *Historical Criticism of the Bible: Methodology or Ideology?* Baker, Michigan, 1992. Until she was converted, Eta Linnemann was an adherent of the radical Bultmann school of biblical criticism.

16. F. F. Bruce, *1 and 2 Thessalonians,* Word, England, 1986, pp.47-9.

17. F. F. Bruce, *Paul: Apostle of the Free Spirit,* Paternoster, Exeter, 1977, p.346.

18. M. Luther, *Lectures on Romans,* trans by W. Pauck, Westminster Press, Philadelphia, 1969, p.261.

19. W. Harrington, *Jesus and Paul: Signs of Contradiction,* Michael Glazier Inc, Delaware, 1987, pp.150,160.

20. W. Klassen, 'Musonius Rufus, Jesus, and Paul: Three First-Century Feminists' in *From Jesus to Paul,* p.204.

21. Cited in R. M. Grant, 'Marcion and the Critical Method' in *From Jesus to Paul,* p.208.

22. Cited in C. E. B. Cranfield, *The Gospel according to St Mark,* Cambridge University Press, Cambridge, 1977, p.464.

23. Klassen, 'Musonius Rufus, Jesus and Paul,' p.204.

24. *Ibid.,* p.198.

25. Albert Schweitzer, *The mysticism of Paul the Apostle,* A. & C. Black, London, 1967, p.113.

### Chapter 2 — Paul's view of his own authority

1. Cited in R. N. Longenecker, *The Ministry and Message of Paul,* Zondervan, Michigan, 1976, p.23.

2. C. H. Spurgeon, *Autobiography: The Early Years,* vol. 1, Banner of Truth, Edinburgh, 1976, p.363.

3. Charles Wesley's 'Lord from whom all blessings flow' in *Christian Hymns,* Evangelical Movement of Wales, 1977, no. 353.

4. A. Dallimore, *George Whitefield,* vol. 2, Banner of Truth, Edinburgh, 1980, p.343.

5. J. Calvin, *Commentaries on the Epistles to Timothy, Titus, and Philemon,* trans. by William Pringle, Baker, Michigan, reprinted 1979, p.353.

6. C. S. Lewis, *Mere Christianity,* Collins, Glasgow, reprinted 1975, p.187.

7. W. Hendriksen, *Philippians,* Banner of Truth, Edinburgh, 1973, p.177.

8. J. Calvin, *Commentary on the Epistles of Paul the Apostle to the Corinthians,* trans. by John Pringle, Baker, Michigan, reprinted 1979, p.228.

## Chapter 3 — Paul's knowledge of Jesus' life

1. R. Bultmann, *Theology of the New Testament,* vol. 1, SCM, London, 1965, p.188.
2. J. Gresham Machen, *The Virgin Birth of Christ,* Guardian Press, Michigan, reprinted 1975, p.259.
3. *Ibid.,* p.260.
4. G. Bornkamm, *Paul,* Harper and Row, New York, 1971, p.238.
5. J. Weiss, *Paul and Jesus,* Harper and Brothers, London, 1909, p.53.
6. Martin Hengel, *Between Jesus and Paul,* SCM, London, 1983, p.53.
7. M. Hengel, *The Pre-Christian Paul,* SCM, London, 1991, p.24.

## Chapter 4 — Paul's knowledge of Jesus' words

1. Bultmann, *Theology of the New Testament,* p.35.
2. S. G. Wilson, 'From Jesus to Paul: The Contours and Consequences of a Debate' in *From Jesus to Paul,* p.8.
3. D. Wenham, 'Paul's Use of the Jesus Tradition: Three Samples' in D. Wenham, *Gospel Perspectives: The Jesus Tradition Outside the Gospels,* JSOT Press, Sheffield, 1984, p.9.
4. The word 'broken' may not be authentic. Christ's bones were not broken (John 19:33,36).
5. 'The First Epistle of Clement to the Corinthians (2)', in M. Staniforth (trans), *Early Christian Writings,* Penguin, Harmondsworth, 1972.
6. E. E. Ellis, *Paul's Use of the Old Testament,* Baker, Michigan, 1985, pp.11-12.
7. *Ibid.,* p.14.

## Chapter 5 — Echoes of Jesus' words

1. J. Jeremias, *Unknown Sayings of Jesus,* SPCK, London, 1957, p.90.
2. L. Morris, *The Epistles of Paul to the Thessalonians,* IVP, London, 1974, pp.105-6.
3. C. E. B. Cranfield, *A Critical and Exegetical Commentary on the Epistle to the Romans,* T. & T. Clark, Edinburgh, 1979, p.712.
4. See M. Thompson, *Clothed with Christ: The Example and Teaching of Jesus in Romans 12:1-15:13,* JSOT Press, Sheffield, 1991, pp.180-3.
5. Cranfield, *Commentary on Romans,* p.802.
6. C. Hodge, *A Commentary on 1 & 2 Corinthians,* Banner of Truth, Edinburgh, reprinted 1974, pp.483-8.
7. P. E. Hughes, *Paul's Second Epistle to the Corinthians,* Eerdmans, Michigan, 1975, pp.164-5.
8. *Ibid.,* p.164.

9. D. M. Lloyd-Jones, *Romans: An Exposition of Chapter 6, The New Man,* Banner of Truth, Edinburgh, 1975, p.241.

10. S. Sandmel, 'Parallelomania' in *Journal of Biblical Literature,* vol. LXXXI, March, 1962, p.1.

11. D. C. Allison, Jr, 'The Pauline Epistles and the Synoptic Gospels: The Pattern of the Parallels' in *New Testament Studies,* vol. 28, 1982, p.30, n.100.

12. Cited in W. Barclay, *Educational Ideas in the Ancient World,* Baker, Michigan, 1974, p.78.

13. Cited in D. Dungan, *The Sayings of Jesus in the Churches of Paul,* Basil Blackwell, Oxford, 1971, p.xxii.

## Chapter 6 —The basic gospel in Paul and Jesus

1. F. G. Bratton, 'Continuity and Divergence in the Jesus-Paul Problem' in *Journal of Biblical Literature,* vol. 48, 1929, p.151.

2. Harrington, *Jesus and Paul,* p.33.

3. S. G. Wilson in *From Jesus to Paul,* p.11.

4. Harrington, *Jesus and Paul,* p.189.

5. C. E. Raven, *St Paul and the Gospel of Jesus,* SCM, London, 1961, p.22.

6. B. E. Thiering, *Jesus the Man,* Doubleday, Sydney, 1992. Dr Thiering claims that Jesus had two sons, because Acts 6:7 and 12:24 say that the word increased! Also when Acts 16:14 says that the Lord opened the heart of Lydia, it means that Jesus and Lydia fell in love. There is much more in the same vein; the result is a peculiar combination of the bizarre and the blasphemous.

7. Wrede, *Paul,* p.151.

8. See W. Bousset, *Kyrios Christos,* Abingdon, Nashville, reprinted 1970.

9. *Ibid.,* p.182.

10. Wrede, *Paul,* pp.163-4.

11. Weiss, *Paul and Jesus,* p.13.

12. Harrington, *Jesus and Paul,* p.39.

13. *Ibid.,* p.40.

14. *Ibid.,* p.41.

15. L. Morris, *The Apostolic Preaching of the Cross,* IVP, Leicester, 1976, p.143.

16. A. M. Hunter, *Paul and his Predecessors,* SCM, London, 1960, p.96.

17. D. Cairns, *The Image of God in Man,* Collins, London, 1973, p.283.

## Chapter 7 — Aspects of the Christian life in Jesus and Paul

1. C. S. Lewis, *Prayer: Letters to Malcolm,* Fontana, Glasgow, 1977, p.119.
2. Cited in A. Vidler, *20th Century Defenders of the Faith,* SCM, London, 1965, p.42. This book is sadly mistitled.
3. Cited in E. R. Norman, *The Victorian Christian Socialists,* Cambridge University Press, Cambridge, 1987, p.7.
4. C. H. H. Scobie, 'Jesus or Paul? The Origin of the Universal Mission of the Christian Church' in *From Jesus to Paul,* p.56.
5. M. Bonar (ed), *Andrew Bonar: Diary and Life,* Banner of Truth, Edinburgh, reprinted 1984, p.358.
6. Robert Murray M'Cheyne's 'When this passing world is done' in *The Church Hymnary Revised Edition,* Oxford University Press, London, 1929, no. 582.
7. B. Pascal, *Pensées,* Penguin, Harmondsworth, reprinted 1973, p.222.
8. John Newton's 'Approach, my soul, the mercy-seat' in *The Church Hymnary, Revised Edition,* no. 451.
9. M. Loane, *John Charles Ryle, 1816-1900,* Hodder and Stoughton, London, 1983, p.113.

## Chapter 8 — Paul and the other apostles

1. L. Gaston, 'Paul and Jerusalem' in *From Jesus to Paul,* p.71.
2. C. H. Dodd, *The Apostolic Preaching and its Developments,* Hodder and Stoughton, London, 1936, p.26.
3. Eusebius, *The History of the Church,* Penguin, Harmondsworth, 1984, p.152.
4. In Acts 14:14 Barnabas is called an apostle too.
5. James Adamson, *The Epistle of James,* Eerdmans, Michigan, 1977, p.68.
6. See R. H. Gundry, '"*Verba Christi*" in 1 Peter: their implications concerning the authorship of 1 Peter and the authenticity of the Gospel tradition' in *New Testament Studies,* vol. 13, July 1967, pp.336-50.

## Chapter 9 — Paul as Christ's ambassador

1. G. Bornkamm, *presbeuo* in G. Kittel and G. Friedrich (eds), *Theological Dictionary of the New Testament,* abridged in one volume by G. W. Bromiley, Eerdmans/Paternoster, Michigan/Exeter, 1985, p.935.